Achieving Brilliance at Home

HOW TO TEACH YOUR CHILD ALMOST ANYTHING

Jeanne Mifflin

*Peaches,
Your brilliance
is showing
Jeanne Mifflin*

Copyright © 2012 by Jeanne Mifflin

All rights reserved. No part of this book may be reproduced or transmitted in any form or by any means, electronic or mechanical, including photocopying, recording, or by any information storage or retrieval system, without written permission from Jeanne Mifflin, except for brief quotations in a review.

Illustrations by Jeanne Mifflin unless otherwise noted.

Printed in the United States of America

ISBN-10: 1477468110

ISBN-13: 978-1477468111

First Edition

Achieving Brilliance at Home

This book is dedicated to parents who delight in raising their children.

Tybee Island, GA

Jeanne Mifflin

SPECIAL NOTE

The information contained in this book is intended to complement, not substitute for, the advice of your child's pediatrician, teacher, school system, therapist or other recognized professional. Before attempting any of the activities outlined in this book, discuss the appropriateness of the activity for your specific child with any professional that is in charge of oversight of your child's education. In addition, not all activities are appropriate for all children at all developmental levels. Your good judgment and discretion is required in evaluating potential activities for your child.

Even though I strongly encourage parents to learn how to teach their child new skills, if you find that you are struggling with drug, alcohol, tobacco, anger management, domestic abuse, mental illness, medical incapacitation or other serious personal problems, it is genuinely recommended that you allow the school system to continue to educate your child completely and that you address these problems directly before attempting increased interaction with your child.

Before attempting any of the undertakings shown in this book, determine whether you might need an assistant to help you (as may the case with some of the infant activities).

Contents

Heart of Brilliance 10

Soul of Brilliance 12

I. SPIRIT OF BRILLIANCE 14

Approach 14

Advantages 15

Afraid to Teach 16

Attaining Independence 21

Ability to Teach 22

Awareness of Progress 24

Avoiding Discouragement 25

II. FOUNDATION OF BRILLIANCE 27

Gateways to Learning 27

Goal Setting 29

General Guidelines.. 30
Giving Directions... 32
Guide to Bedroom Cleaning.. 33
Games for Time Management.. 34
General to Detailed Lesson Creation 35
Green Lesson Trees 37
Greatest Danger.. 41
Genuine Teaching Materials 41

III. ILLUMINATION OF BRILLIANCE 43

Evaluate Your Child's Curriculum 44
Educational Jargon.. 44
Educational Acronyms and Vocabulary............................. 45
Exercise Good Judgment... 51
Emphasize the Most Important 52
Enquiry Schedule... 58

IV. BIRTH OF BRILLIANCE 60

Things to Come 61
Tips for Six Months to a Year... 63
Tricks for One to Three Year Olds 68
Techniques for Three to Seven Year Olds 75

V. ANIMATION OF BRILLIANCE 88

Special Thoughts 89
Secret Behavior Monitoring.. 91
Selective Reward Ideas 95
Safe Consequences.. 97

Schedule for Very Young Children 98
Supplementary Skills 99
Summer Schedule Example 101

VI. CAPTIVATION OF BRILLIANCE 102
Cross-Referencing Materials 102
Creating Your Own Materials 103
Customizing Viewing Reels 108
Cross-Subject Inclusive Green Lesson Tree 108

VII. MATHEMATICS OF BRILLIANCE 111
Alice in Wonderland & Problem Solving 112
African Safari Rescue & Decimal Quest 125
Valley of the Kings & The Geometry Curse 141
Alien Sock Hop & Martian Measurement 153
Last Amazon Tribe & Probability and Statistics 166
Greek Mythology & The Hercules Fraction Flip 185

VIII. WINGS OF BRILLIANCE 199
Free Fun 199
Focus on the Library 200
Frequent Store Outings 201
Fabulous Holidays 202
Fanciful Party Ideas 202
Field Trips 203
Fun Ideas from Theme Parks 204

IX. FAMILY OF BRILLIANCE 207
Is Homeschooling an Option? 208

What are My Legal Requirements? 213
How Do I Put Together a Portfolio? 215
What Do I Teach? 216
What About My Child With Special Needs? 218

ABOUT THE AUTHOR 220

Introduction

The traditional family lifestyle of a loving (yet restrained) spirit in the home, well-planned meals and cleanliness, a good education, church attendance and wholesome free-time activities remains as the best possible foundation in giving your child a good start in life. This lifestyle is also the easiest and most fun to achieve.

New ideas invite all the family's personalities to have fun while discovering the extraordinary in ordinary daily life. Easy routines beckon children to provide the same special care to other family members that Mom gives them all the time.

Home comforts, such as clean and pleasant surroundings, comfortable seating and good lighting, a suitably warmed or cooled room or an outdoor fresh air location, special writing implements, adequate supplies, appropriate breaks and personal Teacher's Pet attention, offer an exemplary setting for teaching. When you teach your child difficult subjects in a unique and refreshingly fun way, you can transform learning into a wonderful experience for you both.

Field trips filled with thrilling activities, memories about which to daydream, and step-by-step learning expectations are enjoyable for all children and substitute for extravagant, expensive and educationally-void amusements.

Do you want to equip your family with a spirit of approval, encouragement, mutual friendship, and ever-expanding creativity? Learning to entertain and educate your child yourself is the very best way for them to get the very best start in life and develop the very best friendship with you. Good luck on your wonderful journey.

Jeanne Mifflin

Heart of Brilliance

This list reveals what your child will need to learn quickly:

Learning to Speak	Matching pictures to real life objects
	Naming toys and parts of things
	Acting Out/Saying new vocabulary verbs
	Acting out play scenarios using toys, tools and other available resources
	Listening to/Creating music CDs
	Watching/Creating DVDs
	Learning/Singing songs
	Learning/Reciting rhymes and poems
	Learning phonics for reading
Using Your Hands	Push, pull, twist, pour, tear, spoon, tong, tie, button, zip, snap, clothes pin, etc.
	Computer mouse
	Imitate lines, circles, shapes
	Draw
	Cut with scissors
	Write letters and sentences (as child is learning phonics)
	Learn to type (summer months)
Using Your Body	Push up on forearms from tummy, roll over backwards and forwards, pull up to standing, sit up, crawl, stand, walk, run, hop, jump, kick, climb, tiptoe, gallop, skip
	Push/Pull, carry, hit, throw, catch

Achieving Brilliance at Home

Reading	Restaurant and trade logos
	Consonant sounds
	Vowels and most common sounds
	Simple rhyming words – cat, bat, hat
	Sight words (ongoing)
	Combined consonants – ch, th, sh
	Vowel sounds and combinations
	Listening to Your New Reader Read for 20 Minutes a Day
	Comprehension (ongoing)
	Grammar
Math	Counting, skip counting, place counting
	Addition, subtraction, multiplication, division
	Fractions, geometry, decimals, probability and statistics, measurement, word problems
Social Studies	Community – fireman, policeman, teachers, post office, etc.
	Ancient civilizations
	American history
	World history and cultures
	Economics and government
Science	Universe & Planets (emphasis on Earth)
	Living and Nonliving things
	Machines
	Scientific method and scientists

Please note that the above list is a general overview only.

Jeanne Mifflin

<u>Soul of Brilliance</u>

1. **What special resources does my family have that I can use to teach my child** – library, swimming pool, close family, lots of toys, siblings, nearby park, museum close by, etc.?
2. **What is my child particularly good at?**
3. **What does my child have the most trouble with?**
4. **What do I think is the greatest risk to my child's future** and will them help them somewhat overcome or better cope with this danger?

> **Teach Them Now *or* Take Care of Them Later**

What <u>exactly</u> do I want my child to learn? (Curriculum)

I promise to review or prepare my materials in advance. I will:

- Show them how I do it using prepared toys, games and other activities,
- Help them do it several times,
- Let them practice doing it the way I showed them,
- See if they can do it when they are alone, and
- Give them more practice opportunities so that they can experience the feeling of ease and success.

If they are not learning, I will ask myself:

- Do they have the foundation skills needed to learn this new task? In other words, make sure they can skip count easily before you try to teach them to multiply.
- Is it a work problem or a routine problem?

- Did I use materials or rewards that they like enough to work for or did I use what was on sale?
- Did I teach them what they know are supposed to do and to what standard?
- Did I come up with a checklist to give them a goal to aim for in order to complete this group of tasks?

I will write down their behavior for at least one day and review it for patterns and changes I could make to support positive responses to my requests. Is there a main problem that other problems spin off of such as:

- Hunger?
- Time of day?
- Type of work?
- Materials used for teaching?

> **What does my mother's intuition say about the problem?**

If it's a behavior problem, I will:

- Stick to my planned routine,
- Not be caught off guard by fussing, whining and tantrums and I will allow lots of extra time during the first two weeks for these new schedule behaviors,
- Supply promised rewards for good work, along with lots of praise and enthusiasm, the *moment* they begin to behave well (but after they've finished the job), and
- No TV, computer, or whatever happens to be their favorite leisure time activity unless they worked for me through learning.

Jeanne Mifflin

Georgia Aquarium, Atlanta, GA

I. Spirit of Brilliance

The Spirit of Brilliance encompasses your approach and many other abilities that you will need to resource within yourself. This chapter will help you with the following:

- Your approach to teaching your child,
- What you can expect of yourself as a new teacher,
- Acknowledging progress,
- Avoiding discouragement,
- Overcoming your fears, and
- Examining the differences in how children learn.

Approach

Getting to know your own child's interests and abilities is a wonderful opportunity in today's world. So many parents have missed it. To know another person deeply is a great privilege – for it to be your child reveals a treasure chest of wonderful memories.

You will come to know all of your child interests and will be aware of when they change as they grow. Specific detailed and personally tested information will enable you to stand up to professionals and/or pinpoint more exactly any problems.

As you are teaching your child, remember that God is teaching you in the process. Know that you are also loved and cared for and have not been forgotten. Everything is working out as planned.

Never be ashamed of taking delight in your child and his milestones and accomplishments. Your job is to create a beautiful life for you and your family and to enjoy all of the wonders of your home. For that, you don't have to be the richest or the prettiest or the thinnest or the tallest. You just have to be you! Your son doesn't have to be the smartest or the most athletic or the most handsome, he just has to express the wonder within himself!

Advantages

As you travel along in your new undertaking, you will gain confidence in working with your child and be able to teach them important life skills that they can, in turn, teach your grandchildren one day. Your home life will be enhanced by shared knowledge. A mother's insight will guide you when making decisions for a special needs child and you can make sure that they continue to progress (regardless of the skill level of their teacher).

Your older children will be rewarded with a mother who can help them with their homework all throughout their school years. This may well keep them from falling behind in school.

Family excursions and activities for your gifted child will complement the opportunities provided them by their school. In the process of learning to teach them, you will develop a special friendship with and enjoyment of your child (just as school teachers often do).

Don't be surprised if your spouse begins to gain an understanding, as well, of how children learn and you may be surprised to discover that he has an interest in and talent for teaching your children new skills.

Ensuring your children's Christian education is a major benefit of knowing how your children learn and how to teach them these Biblical life skills yourself. It also assures that you can work on these lessons together as a family.

Afraid to Teach

There are many reasons why we may be fearful of teaching our children anything. The following are pretty common in our society:

- Bad childhood memories of our parents trying to teach us new skills,
- Fear of ridicule from others,
- Fear of ridicule from professional teachers,
- Fear we will teach them the wrong way,
- Intimidated by teaching language,
- Uneasy feeling of lack of focus and organizational skills,
- Behavior difficulties,
- Pressure to be a "loving" and undemanding mother,
- Time, money and energy,
- Home problems such as money and marital concerns, and
- Lack of a college degree.

Let's take a closer look at these problems:

- **Bad childhood memories of our parents trying to teach us new skills,**

Surprisingly, parents have never really been equipped with the necessary skills to teach their children, but have been held to the highest expectations *for* teaching their children. This book hopes to provide at least the basics. Don't worry; you *will* do better than your parents did with you (if you follow the common sense guidelines set out in this book).

- **Fear of ridicule from others,**

Whenever you try something different, expect to be ridiculed. Consider it a form of flattery. Yes, you are going to be different – you are going to be better. Don't tell anyone if it's truly a problem. Just merrily work with your child, as if it's a natural part of your parenting style, and no one may notice. If someone really tries to sit you down and "set you straight" (and inhibit you and your child's ability to grow), just let them have their say (but don't you dare take it to heart). Do the right thing – you're not confused – you know the truth of the situation in your heart.

- **Fear of ridicule from professional teachers,**

They won't know if you don't tell them. Don't expect them to encourage you in any way except to go to college and get a degree (if you don't already have one). They will not appreciate it that you're teaching your child so don't go looking for affirmation from them.

- **Fear we will teach them the wrong way,**

Yes, you may actually make a few (or a lot) of mistakes in the beginning. Guess what, first year teachers are notorious for making mistakes. It takes a teacher several years to become a good teacher (and that's if she really *wants* to be a good teacher) even though *she teaches the same lessons every year.* *You* will not have that ability. *You* will have to keep pace with your child's changing coursework every year.. If you're still a bad teacher after five years of sincere effort teaching your own child, then, okay, you're just not cut out for teaching.

- **Intimidated by educational jargon,**

Professional teaching resources and education web sites are filled with specialized jargon that reduces down to very simple concepts and ideas. I hope to cut through much of that for you in this book.

- **Uneasy feeling of lack of focus and organizational skills,**

Organizing skills are a key ingredient of successful teaching. Buy a book or curriculum to help you get started in the beginning if you need help. I suggest this anyway as a great timesaving measure. Study your purchased materials while your child is attending school and do the activities on the weekends or as homework (if they have a light homework schedule). If your child already has a heavy homework schedule, (1) they are being taught well at school and the homework truly does reinforce what they are learning, or (2) they are not learning at school and you are doing the teaching at home anyway (whether you realize it or not).

- **Behavior difficulties,**

This is the most common reason a parent is reluctant to try and teach their child and will be discussed in much detail later in this book.

- **Societal pressure to be a "loving" and "undemanding" mother,**

There has been much discussion about the need for a mother to be loving, nurturing, warm, servant-like, undemanding and inexhaustible at all times and under all circumstances. Nonsense! No human being alive could pull that off! Your goal (in addition to loving them and taking care of their physical needs) is to teach your child all the skills they will need to attain independence from you one day. They will not find the qualities previously listed in any teacher, boss, police officer, doctor, spouse or other person they encounter during their entire lifetime.

You want to teach your child to live in the real world instead of sacrificing yourself to create a false one from which they may never escape. I'm assuming that, if you're reading this book, you probably have the love part down pat. This book will give you tips on how to learn to teach your child so that they become independent. This book will also help you emerge from the baby and toddler years (where you really do often have to cater to the physical and emotional needs of the child) with a set of instructions as to how to proceed so that your family doesn't get caught in a dependency net for a lifetime.

- **Time, money and energy,**

Be realistic about what you can do. Don't pull your kids out of school because they're having difficulty if you're not sure you can devote the time and energy to teaching them yourself. Practice in the evenings and on weekends to see if you're up to the task first. Research potential money outlays in advance.

- **Home problems such as money and marital concerns, and**

    These problems seem to be ever present in today's society and offer even more incentive for you to learn to teach your child yourself. Once you have acquired the ability to work with your child, you will have a real edge in providing support, security and consistency to your child throughout life's many changes. You will know them well and will know what to target in order to help them cope with any existing situation. You won't have to emotionally abandon your child because you are caught in the backwash of tragedy. Your children will be able to help you with the laundry, housecleaning, meal preparation, and other daily necessities during times of emergency (if you've taught them how to do these things when all was going well).

- **Lack of a college degree.**

    A college degree would be wonderful. At the very least, it would make it a lot easier to teach your child knowing all of the basics in advance yourself. The modeling of great instructional techniques by top-notch teachers is an extremely valuable advantage (if you had those great teachers in college).

    Don't despair if you don't have a college degree. See this as an opportunity to acquire the education you never received (even if it is never formally recognized). There are wonderful used textbooks available on amazon.com and many textbook manufacturers offer online videos in subjects like math. Some teachers post their own instructional videos on YouTube. Type in a specific phrase such as "fraction to decimal" and see what comes up.

    It's easier to learn on your own today than it has ever been. Just don't try to start at the Seventh Grade level (unless you're actually pretty good at math). Research and learn up to the grade level that you are trying to teach. Go to your state's Board of Education web site to see what is being taught for your child's grade level. See if you can locate fairly current quality textbooks for that subject and grade. Look on the back of the textbook around the bar code for a possible clue as to the grade level.

Attaining Independence

The test of whether you have been a good teacher is whether or not your child can do the task alone (without your assistance). Independence means that your child knows the right thing to do and will do it without help when no one is looking and when no one makes them do the right thing. Future independence is the goal for your child whether it's in being able to take care of themselves, handle money, hold down a job, maintain a home and a car, develop a good working marital relationship or raise (teach) and care for your grandchildren one day.

> **Teach Them Now or
> Take Care of Them Later**

Fortunately, children gain self-control, understanding, and abilities as they age. Unfortunately, many children start tumbling backward educationally in elementary school and never do fully recover. A major goal for you and your child is to keep them on grade level throughout the elementary school years so that, by the time they actually become aware of their place in life in middle school, they are proud of where they happen to find themselves standing.

Learning time is continually racing forward for your child. Don't panic, but make sure your child isn't sitting on the side waving goodbye to all of the other go-karts. Ensure that they are learning during the years they are supposed to be learning (instead of just being babysat) or you will need to teach them yourself. If school serves as a social outlet only for your child and no true learning occurs, you may have to face the difficult decision of whether or not to homeschool your child. Please see the chapter on homeschooling in this book if you would like to explore that lifestyle further.

Ability to Teach

The main job requirements are as follows:

- Self-discipline enough to do the same thing, in the same way, at the same time, every day (except Saturday and Sunday).

- Ability to balance love and warmth with expectation and firmness.

- Ability to give verbal instructions in a very clear and brief way (even if you have to use pictures).

- Willingness to create models for your child. For example, if your child has

**The Same Thing
Done in the Same Way
At the Same Time
Every Day**

trouble coloring, make a copy of the exact sheet he will be coloring and color it together (or even color the picture completely yourself to use as a model). You will say, "Let's color the tree green." You will then color the tree green as your child watches. Your child will then color his tree green. Part of your child's learning curve will involve teaching your child (1) not to grab materials, (2) to watch while you show, and (3) to then perform the action himself.

- No matter how much time and love you put into creating a teaching material for your child, you have to put your feelings aside and try something else if it's not working. Sorry.

- Genuine fun and mutual "like" are the goals as opposed to a sugary "I wonderful" pretentious presentation. You will discover that, as you gain confidence, you will become a nice balance of "firm yet loving" without trying at all. It will become second nature to you. In the meantime, just wrap yourself in the idea of trying to be a good teacher.

You will find that you are unfulfilled if you look for affirmation from people who don't understand or who don't want to understand. Keep your new relationship with your child to yourself until you've gained enough experience to have confidence in both of your abilities. Others may be jealous or misunderstand your intentions.

I'll be going over how to set up a unit and lesson plan in the next chapter, as well as how children learn. Let your very best be good enough. You may discover that you are not well-suited to teaching. Too bad. You will be your child's teacher until they leave home. Teach them well now so that you don't find yourself teaching a 35 year-old.

New material will consist of ideas, abilities or links between related information. How you introduce this material will directly impact whether they learn it or not.

> **Use the Skill and Talent That You Currently Have.**
> **Use the Resources That Are Currently Available.**
> **Achieve Goals That Are Currently Possible.**

Pace yourself according to the amount of time and material that your child can absorb easily in one sitting. Also, build in frequent breaks. Try bouncing a balloon (for a quick break) and, when it hits the floor, break time is over. For younger children, only have 15 minute learning sessions on the hour several times a day.

Awareness of Progress

It is especially important that you pay attention, notice and remark on any progress that you child makes. Their progress is your progress and self-encouragement and encouragement of your child is what's going to get you both through the trouble spots together. During those periods when you feel like you've both stalled out, bring in fresh materials and try a seasonal or holiday change to reinvigorate you both.

Help your child feel successful with their finished work. In the beginning, you will need to tread gently as your child gains confidence and learns how to be critiqued with an attitude of "teach me, please." Once they have enough experience and have learned that what you teach them makes them feel confident, they will become more and more willing to work with you.

Review what your child already knows about a subject before presenting new information. Please don't present yourself to your child as a "professional teacher." Many children would prefer a nice warm mommy that has a sincere desire to help them gain confidence in their own ability.

Tell your child exactly what they do right. Go ahead, make a big fuss over them when they do a good job. After all, they are Teacher's Pet.

Avoiding Discouragement

If you find your family is suffering, for whatever reason, step back and reinforce the fundamentals of health, love, tolerance, discipline, and encouragement. If you're really miserable, the kids are probably in charge. See the chapter in this book that deals with behavior. It will give you lots of information on how to take back your home.

Never blame your child for your own shortcomings. It's time to create a better parenting style. If your child is to blame for all of your problems, then there are no solutions (except for really, really, bad ones). Even if you have a particularly difficult situation and would be pitied by most people, pity offers you no direction or guidance. A spirit of trust and positive expectancy girds your resolve and allows you to walk out of the dark forest of misty uncertainty into the brilliance of the sunlight.

If you ever notice that *you* are starting to tantrum, whine, fuss, complain and take on a negative outlook on your life circumstance, (1) rule out illness or exhaustion, (2) get some physical exercise or rest (as indicated), and (3) switch out your routine a little to reinvigorate yourself. A nice little field trip to the botanical gardens might be in order here. Perhaps a trip to the beach? Picnic in the backyard? You get the idea.

As you and your child uncover areas of difficulty, make sure you don't use the hammers of sarcasm, shame, guilt, hate or fear to channel your frustrations. Don't fall victim to the evil of these devices. Take a deep breath, say to yourself, "I'm not going to let this situation steal away my love for my child and my respect for myself." Think to yourself, "I'm doing the best I can, my child is doing the best he can, and our life situation is exactly the way it is supposed to be -- nothing is wrong." Sometimes, you will need to give you and your child a breather to break the tension. That's okay. I want you to learn how to be as firm as possible with your child, but I also want you to learn to recognize when you need to utilize a last minute escape hatch.

Don't worry about missed opportunities. You are the important appointment for your child. No matter how much your child and your family may have missed or been denied, you are the determining factor as to whether your child will succeed.

If you do find that you've become discouraged, focus on creating new ways of teaching a lesson rather than destroying all the work you've already done with your child.

Frustration is natural on both parts. It simply signals that you need to step back and look at the situation yet again with fresh eyes. It is very important that you get to know your child as he really is as opposed to the way you wish he had turned out. It is also time to make friends with who you are instead of who you thought you would be or who other people told you that you should be.

Prayer works well when you are especially in need of inspiration. This does require a sincere prayer and enough trust and faith to leave the matter with God at least overnight (if not for a weekend). Somehow, for me, inspiration always comes if you trust and release.

II. Foundation of Brilliance

This chapter will tell you about how children learn, how to set goals and create your own lessons, and specifics as to how to teach your child. You will also learn how to check the effectiveness of the teaching materials that you create yourself.

Gateways to Learning

There are fine books on the market that describe the differing ways that children learn and preferred activities for each style. I'm providing you with a brief overview on the following pages, but it's a good idea to do additional research to the extent that you can pinpoint your own child's learning preferences. Look for books that have titles with words like "learning styles" and "multiple intelligences."

Eyes	Child likes to learn through watching demonstrations, videos, or other people; reading posters and instructional drawings; and anything with colorful pictures is usually a plus.
Ears	Child likes to learn through music and songs, listening to people talk, and rhythmic sounds.
Mouth	Interactive discussion is the way this child loves to learn.
Hands	Never "do" for this child. He's the one who needs to be the "doing" or he will not learn. You show him how to do it (in small easy steps that build on each other) and then immediately have him do it. Using as few words as possible is required to teach this child.
Movement	Stillness makes this child uncomfortable and it's helpful if you can combine learning with movement. For example, have him toss a medium sized plastic ball (like they have in ball pits) for every letter (preferably with the letter and associated photo and word shown on the ball) as he says his ABCs and he will learn them easier.
Thought	Child likes to ponder and come up with his own solutions. Give him a problem to work out and let him come up with his own ideas. For example, teach him about planting a garden and then let him decide the process steps and garden plant arrangement.
Alone	Child prefers to learn in a solitary or one-on-one environment.
Group	Lots of interaction and group activity brings out the best in this child.

In a school environment, your child must adapt to the environment and the resources that are available so don't be disappointed if you can't change your child's teacher or the school. You can, however, work with your child at home in their preferred learning mode as additional reinforcement of what they're learning in school.

Goal Setting

Decide what you need to teach and by what date you want your child to have learned the material. Setting high *appropriate* goals establishes high expectations (once you've discovered your child's current true educational levels through experimentation).

Make sure that everything you teach is related to your goal and that you don't get sidetracked by resource books or your student's whims. Follow teaching with workbooks or homework to see if your child can transfer what they learned. (If he can't, do the same worksheet every day or dry erase the final test every day and build upon his learning that way.)

Start with the easiest and work your way up with as much repetition and review as needed. Teach a theme in each subject area at the same time if at all possible. For example, a theme on the Amazon rain forests might include writing (Language Arts) a research paper on the animals that live there (science), watching a video on the native cultures that live in the Amazon basin or studying a map of the area (social studies), reading fiction and nonfiction stories about the Amazon (Reading) and math (Math) that somehow relates to the Amazon rain forest (see chapter entitled, "Last Amazon Tribe & Probability and Statistics," for ideas).

Do learning activities teach exactly what you targeted to teach? Are they fun and enjoyable for your child? If your child is getting frustrated because what you put together to make learning fun for them is not working, let it go and move on to what will work.

Triple check to make sure that all activities are appropriate in regard to your child's academic level and preferred learning style.

Be sure to match your activities to what your child will actually be tested on to show that they have learned what you tried to teach them.

General Guidelines

You will push your child along to perform new skills, but only after you have a good feel for what they can do easily. To

> **Never restrict your child to age or grade level. Find out where they actually are and work from there.**

determine your child's current academic level, locate a few online activities (www.gamequarium.com) that correlate to what your child is supposed to be learning. (See the curriculum pages in the next chapter of this book.)

Adjust your expectations if your child has difficulty with the activity. It's one thing to take the time to familiarize them with a web site and/or an activity. It's another thing for them to be clueless and frustrated as to how to perform an activity. If it's too hard, back it up (even to an earlier grade or age level). If it's too easy, jump ahead. Don't be surprised if you discover that your child needs to review some subjects and advance more quickly in others.

> ***Restroom Warning:*** Make sure your child goes to the restroom *before* you sit down to teach them anything. There is no greater frustration than to be finally seated at the table, have the teaching materials laid out in readiness, you have just carefully gone over all of the instructions and your child has just repeated them back to you, and then your child suddenly says, "I need to go to the bathroom."

Always try to fill in any gaps you may encounter in your child's education. That said, don't bring the world to a stop just because your child doesn't quite have it yet. Keep working on it, but don't get stuck there. If your child is becoming frustrated and disruptive, that's a major problem and you are better off moving on to something at which he *can* feel successful and then returning to the problem area a little later.

Know that there will be problems. The true task is in coming up with creative ways to teach your child and learning activities that they will enjoy. Make sure that the work is not too difficult and that you are not trying to start on "grade level" for a child who is running behind. Get to know your child well enough to anticipate the types of problems he/you will have and to plan for them ahead of time.

Expect that there will be times when you'll be going along just fine and, suddenly, the learning comes to an outright stop. You realize that your child is going to need a lot more instruction, activity and practice in order to master this particular skill. No problem, this book is loaded with ideas to get you unstuck and there are also many books available at teacher supply stores. Look for the phrases, "learning center," or, "multisensory." As a general rule, they will be the most helpful resources but you will need to put the materials together in advance.

Don't guess at subject matter. Buy a curriculum, textbook, or thoroughly research the subject yourself.

Giving Directions

Your instructions to your child need to very clear and easy to understand. Try to anticipate mis-understandings, based upon your knowledge of your child, and make your directions especially clear in those areas. As a general rule, the fewer well-chosen words, the better.

> **The Fewer, Well-Chosen, Words, The Better**

Speak well, write well, and expand your own vocabulary. Your child will imitate you in these areas (whether you want them to or not). When you read your child a storybook, try to act out the personalities of the characters. Imagine a movie star that you are very familiar with and superimpose his or her voice and mannerisms upon the storybook character. Of course you can't do it perfectly - that just makes it more fun!

Have your child repeat any directions back to you. If they become confused, restate your directions as (1) first task stated in 3-5 words, (2) second task stated in 3-5 words, and (3) final task stated in 3-5 words. Test to see if your child understands the directions now. If they are still having trouble, state the first task in 3-5 words and let them perform that alone, completely, before moving on to the next task.

Give your child a pause to think (about 5 seconds) before he answers your questions unless you're working with flash cards. If he speaks off task, restate your question and ask again until he responds (if he has the language capacity to understand what you are asking). If he truly doesn't understand, use pictures and even 2-3 word questions.

If your child is having language difficulties, you'll want to focus on teaching him noun words for the things that he likes and uses daily and verbs that are easy for him to act out. You will use these simple noun-verb combinations to help him learn to express his needs.

For flash cards, you will want your child to come in under 3-5 seconds and you can tap out the time, use a timer of some type, or even a stop watch to make it more fun and exciting. If your child becomes frustrated, extend the time in which they have to answer the question and gradually reduce it as they get better.

> **Your child performs all the action such pouring, handling, reading and writing** unless you're giving them an initial demonstration which they will repeat immediately after you.

Guide to Bedroom Cleaning

Don't ever attempt to teach your child by giving them a big mess to straighten out. Don't tell your child to go "clean their room" when you haven't organized or cleaned it in a year yourself. First, organize, clean up and take a "before" picture of the room which you have cleaned to your standards.

List the steps you took in order to clean their room on a card you can post next to the picture. The steps will probably be things like (1) put all dirty clothes in the hamper, (2) pick up all hangers and put them in the laundry room, (3) put all toys in the toy box, (4) put all books on the bookshelf, (5) make your bed, (6) put the used water glass in the kitchen sink, (7) empty the trash, etc. Repeat: make notes of the steps *you* take to clean their room so that you can post them in your child's room.

If your child tends to play and dawdle, set a timer for 20 minutes and have a prescribed reward for having it done before the timer goes off. For example, you may reward your child for a clean room with 20 minutes of their favorite activity.

If you see that your child is trying, but it's just too big a job, you can either (1) break the job into parts and cycle it as 20 minutes of cleaning for 20 minutes of free time, (2) tell them that it's too big a job, that they still get their reward, and that you will do it together over several Saturdays, or (3) tell them that you will take care of it yourself and then they will only be expected to keep it straight on Saturdays morning before they get to watch cartoons.

If your child does not read yet, you will need to take pictures of them performing specific tasks. For example, you might take a picture of your child placing a dirty shirt in the clothes hamper. You will take appropriate pictures for each step you want them to perform. You will then combine all photos into a poster for their bedroom. Be sure and print out the steps wording, as well, so that you can say the steps in the same way every time.

You will point to the picture of the task, walk your child through the task (as many times as needed), and then let your child perform the task solo with you watching. You are going to have the thrill of your life one day when you tell your child to "go clean up your room" and you are amazed to discover that it's actually been done (even if it's not up to designer mommy standards).

Games for Time Management

Never leave your child sitting with nothing to do while you are preparing the lesson or "getting ready." Have a theme-related instructional video, educational computer game or book set aside for them to look at when they have to wait.

Use cue words or cue circumstances to let your child know when and if you want them to react immediately. For example, "now" is a strong word used to mean immediately. In the beginning, if your child does not respond, you will repeat your request and the word "now" and then (gently but firmly) guide their body through the activity you wanted them to do (such as pick up their books and papers off the floor).

They usually get the idea right away, when they're still very young, and will respond to "now" immediately forever after. It also helps if you turn off the TV (even if the rest of the family groans) until your request has been completed. You might even want to get the other people present to perform a quick task as well.

"Cue circumstances" can also serve you well. For example, you can play a game with your child whereby you allow them to get dressed for daytime or bedtime during the commercials of their favorite TV show. As they get older, when you want them to do a chore, you can use the "do it during the commercial" game. If they refuse to comply, you simply turn the TV off or make them go to their bedroom (where there is no TV or internet). They may fuss this time, but they will know better for next time.

Always plan the next activity to help motivate your child through. For example, instead of saying, "Hurry and get dressed," add, "First, we're going to the doctor's office; then, we're going to the park; after that, we're going to the grocery store; and, when we get home, we'll all have ice cream." If your child really likes ice cream, you're set for the day.

With younger children, you will limit telling them your travel plans to one or two stops. Be sure to plan something they *like* into your plans, if at all possible, to help buy compliance. Just make sure that you get what you need *first*.

General to Detailed Lesson Creation

In this section, you'll learn how to set up a simple lesson and how to begin the process of teaching your child. You're going to be so proud of yourself and your child. It will be hard for you to imagine how your family every functioned before you acquired your new teaching skills.

It is very common, in the beginning, to have many false starts and do overs. This is perfectly normal and you should not allow yourself to become discouraged. Just allow yourself plenty of extra time and self-encouragement in the beginning to learn. This works particularly well if you give your child lots of extra cushion as well. However, once you designate a new routine, it is very important that you follow it for at least two weeks in order to establish the basics. No need to do this in a military fashion, but you will need to do it in a self-disciplined fashion. This will set the example for your child and let them know that you're serious about your new start together.

Build Your Lessons Like a Tree

Leaves (Activities)

Small Branches (Skill or Idea)

Large Branches (Main Subjects)

Tree Trunk (Theme)

(Tree illustration courtesy of www.wallstory-murals.com)

Green Lesson Trees

Build your lessons like a leafy tree (see illustration). Start with the theme (tree trunk). Then, branch out into the main subjects (large branches). Next, branch out into the specific skills or ideas about which you want to teach (smaller branches). Finally, branch out into the activities that you plan to use to teach each skill or idea in a step-by-step manner (leaves).

You will always start with the trunk (theme) and end with the leaves (activities) as you plan out what you want to teach your child. For example, if you want to teach your child words related to home, you would work as is shown on the "Objects Found in the KITCHEN – LESSON 1" illustration that follows.

The illustration gives you a general idea of how I would set up a lesson plan if I wanted to teach a child the names (and uses of) the appliances found in the kitchen. Note that I did not try to teach the child the names of everything in every room of the house on Lesson 1. Please also notice that I did not try to teach the child the names of everything found in the kitchen during Lesson 1. I picked one small branch of the lesson, "Appliances," and then created several activities around that one idea.

If your child picks up the information quickly, you may move on quickly. If your child needs extra time, stay with the *same* lesson until your child is able to do it and starts to feel successful. Praise them abundantly when they succeed.

Jeanne Mifflin

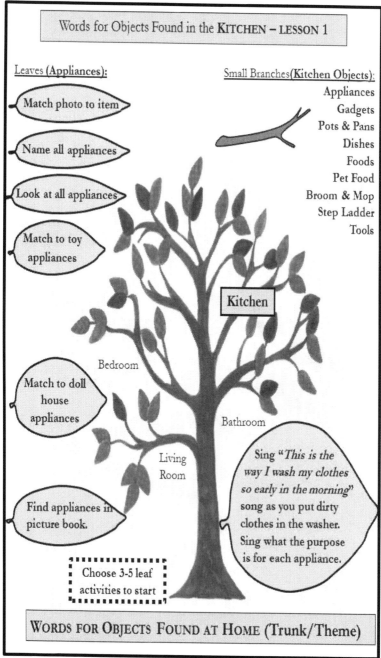

(Tree illustration courtesy of www.wallstory-murals.com)

Rather than just utilizing the activities I used in my leaf illustration, you will review your child's learning preferences and personalize the games and activities for their specific use. Alternative activity options might include:

- Spelling or writing out the words,
- Saying an appliance name (while you and your child are in another room) and having your child run to the correct appliance,
- Assigning an appliance to each child in a group and having the child then tell about their appliance and name the different parts. If this is too easy or if several of the children have trouble, switch the appliance for each child using a timer as in a game of musical chairs,
- or any fun idea that you come up, to which you child will respond, that actually teaches the lesson.

There are many ways to organize your activities. I've listed just a few below to get you started:

- Color, Shape, Size
- Closest to Farthest
- Time Order
- Most Important to Least Important
- Clockwise Order

The Same Thing Done in the Same Way At the Same Time Every Day

If your child is very young or has language difficulties, use very simple and clear wording. For example:

Don't say:

"These are all the appliances that we have in the kitchen — refrigerator, stove, dishwasher, garbage disposal, mixer, blender, toaster, coffee maker and toaster oven," said as you point across the room to each item. "Now, let me tell you what each one does," at which point you face away from your child (so they can't hear you) and touch and talk about each item.

Do say:

"Re-frig-er-a-tor, refrigerator," as you show them a photo of a refrigerator. "Find *same*," said as you hand your child the photo of the refrigerator. If your child stalls, take the card back and say, "re-frig-er-a-tor," as you hold up the photo card in front of your child, and then you tap or touch the card on the refrigerator. Give the card back to your child and say, "Re-frig-er-a-tor, refrigerator." "Find *same*." You may have to back up and work on the words, "same/different" if your child is having language difficulties. Practice using sheets of construction paper or identical pictures. Simply say, "same," or, "different," as you match or mismatch two sheets of construction paper. Stay with the same two colors until your child gets the idea.

Once language starts to come easier for your child, you will begin to add more words (such as a new word each day). You will always review the words your child learned previously before starting a new word. Reinforce this learning whenever you find the specific item as you're reading your child a storybook, watching a video, or happen to see the item in a department store.

Greatest Danger

The greatest danger is in overwhelming your child with information, words, books, pictures, etc. You are going to narrowly focus your teaching to 2-3 words or ideas and then try to explore those in as many ways as possible – just those 2-3. Restraint is crucial. Try it. Did they learn? I thought so.

Genuine Teaching Materials

Whenever your prepare materials for your child, or even when you utilize purchased items, you will need to test their effectiveness against the following criteria:

1. Are they teaching **exactly what you are trying to teach**?
2. Does your child find them fun and engaging?
3. Are they appropriate to your child's level and learning style?
4. Did you start with the easiest and work your way up to harder materials?
5. Did you tie in all the subjects – Reading, Language, Math, Science, Social Studies -- once your child was of Kindergarten age?
6. Did you plan your lesson out from a general theme to a detailed activities (using my Green Lesson Tree format)?
7. Can your child do the activity solo now or are they getting closer each day? Can your child tell you or show you what they learned?
8. Are the behavior issues so bad that you can't seem to really even get your child's attention? If so, please see the chapter on behavior in this book.

You know you have a winning activity when your child is eager to get started. Sometimes, there's a little warm up to the activity. Sometimes, your child screams because they think it looks too hard. Try to show them how fun and easy it is and convince them that they will love it. Sometimes, you just have to go back to the craft and toy areas and come up with something better.

Acting out *Jack & The Bean Stalk*

III. Illumination of Brilliance

In order to illuminate your child's brilliance, you will need to discover their true interests and talents. Learning tasks are exceptionally good ways to reveal your child's special talents and abilities and, as a parent, this information can prove to be invaluable in planning for your child's future.

The most efficient way to coordinate your home and school lessons is to research your state/school's curriculum (what is studied) for your child's current grade and compare it to the paperwork being sent home each day for each subject. If a steady stream of paperwork does not come home with your child (or it is months after the fact), press the teacher for specific details as to what your child is studying. If this doesn't work, you may have to work independently from the school (but be sure and follow your state's curriculum guidelines). Your child may or may not be helpful in providing you with specifics as to what they are learning each day when in school.

Jeanne Mifflin

Evaluate Your Child's Curriculum

In order to work with your child, you will need to be aware of what the curriculum is for your child's grade. Go to your state's Department of Education web site and look for wording like, "curriculum," "standards," "course of study," "frameworks," and "core." You should be able to locate what is taught, in your state, during each grade. You may also want to access your child's commercial testing practice website (such as Study Island) for an overview of what your child is being taught. You can also purchase a curriculum to guide you in teaching your child.

Educational Jargon

Don't be put off by professional educational jargon as the technical wording typically refers to very simple concepts. To give you an idea of how this works, I've provided some examples below:

Educational Jargon	Simple Translation
Identify spheres and cubes.	Find balls and boxes.
Order by size.	Line up by size.
Arrange experiences by sequence.	Tell what you did last weekend by day.
Selects appropriate instrument for determining specific measurement of height, weight, and temperature.	Decide whether to use a tape measure, scale or thermometer for measuring.
Identifies relationships between objects.	Able to say whether something is, "next to," "in front of", etc.

Educational Jargon	Simple Translation
Identifies a compass rose as a directional tool.	Able to point to and know what the N, S, E, W symbol means on a map.
Diphthong	Two vowels together (aw) in the same syllable. (saw)
Digraph	Two consonants (ch) or vowels (ai) together that produce one sound. (chair)

Educational Acronyms and Vocabulary

Useful acronyms and phrases with which you will want to familiarize yourself follow:

Word or Acronym	General or Specific Meaning
accommodations	Changing how something is done in order to help students with special circumstances (such as adding time to a test).
adaptive behavior	Skills that show how well a person can take care of themself.
AP	**A**dvanced **P**lacement – courses designed for children who learn faster.
assessment	test
AYP	**A**dequate **Y**early **P**rogress – whether most of the kids in a school are learning.
benchmark	milestone/progress indicator

Word or Acronym	General or Specific Meaning
charter school	Publicly funded schools that are exempt from many state laws and regulations.
cognitive	mental ability/intelligence
collaborative	working together
competency	ability
CRCT	**C**riterion-**R**eferenced **C**ompetency **T**est – test that measures current knowledge based on what was taught during the school year.
cue	When a hand, picture or word signal is used to show someone what you want them to do.
curriculum	what is going to be taught
declarative sentence	Sentence states information and ends with a period.
differentiation	Changing how something is taught in order to accommodate a child's specific learning needs
ectomorph	A slender body build with little muscular development. (See also "mesomorph".)
endomorph	A heavy, rounded, body build with a tendency to become overweight.
enrichment	Additional work for students who are not being challenged. Can also refer to an enhanced environment such as one with bright colors, many educational toys, etc.

Word or Acronym	General or Specific Meaning
ESL	English as a Second Language – students who are not native English speakers.
ESY	Extended School Year – summer school for students who may lose what they learned over the summer or to catch them up on required work and ability.
exclamatory sentence	Sentence contains strong emotion and ends with an exclamation mark.
expository	writing that explains
FAPE	Free Appropriate Public Education – All children are entitled to a free appropriate public education.
fine motor skills	Skills that involve the use of the small muscles in the body such as when learning to write.
GATE	Gifted and Talented Education
gross motor skills	Skills that involve the use of the large muscles in the body such as when running, bouncing a ball, etc.
IB	International Baccalaureate – high school program for advanced students.
IEP	Individual Education Plan – tool used to plan out special teaching for children with special needs.
imperative sentence	Sentence gives a command and ends with a period.
implement	put into action

Word or Acronym	General or Specific Meaning
integrate	bring parts together to make a whole
interrogative sentence	Sentence asks a questions and ends with a question mark.
intervention	Special help for students who are not learning at the same rate as the other students at their grade level and/or age.
ITBS	**I**llinois **T**est of **B**asic **S**kills – one of many different tests given to students to determine their current knowledge base.
kinesthetic	Used in reference to children who like to learn through hands-on activities.
Language Arts	Reading, writing, listening and speaking
mainstreaming	Placing a special needs child in a classroom with typical children who do not have special needs.
manipulatives	Toys or other items that a child handles in order to understand a specific idea.
mastery	When your child is able to show they have learned based on specific guidelines.
Media Center	school library
mesomorph	A muscular body build.
model	To perform a behavior or skill so that your child can then imitate you.
NCLB	**N**o **C**hild **L**eft **B**ehind – (2002) school performance and accountability standards designed to ensure the adequate education of all American children.

Word or Acronym	General or Specific Meaning
perseverate	To repeat an action over and over again in a determined way.
phonics	A method of teaching a child to read by matching sounds to letters.
proficiency	ability to do something
PTO	**P**arent **T**eacher **O**rganization – helps raise funds based on school needs.
pupil-teacher ratio	The number of students that are in a class as opposed to the number of teachers.
Resource Specialist	Teachers with special teaching certificates that entitle them to work with special education students.
rubric	Outline of the key points on which schoolwork will be graded.
sight words	A list of words expected to be instantly recognized when reading based on grade level.
Special Education	Students with academic or physical obstacles to overcome.
Staff Development Days	Days on which teachers work but students do not go to school.
standardized test	A test that is the same for everyone who takes it.
strategies	Ways that a teacher is going to change *her* teaching, routines, or reactions in order to change a student's learning results.

Word or Acronym	General or Specific Meaning
tenure	After working for a specific amount of time, a teacher is guaranteed employment.
thematic units	Lessons that are built around a theme -- my "Green Lesson Trees" are an example of setting up a thematic unit.
transitions	A child's ability to move from one activity to the next (hopefully, in an uneventful and comfortable way).
whole language	A method of teaching a child to read by focusing on understanding what was read.

As you research your curriculum, note that it breaks down into specific subjects. For therapies, therapist reports and assigned homework will offer the most convenient focus options.

- Reading
- Language Arts
- Writing
- Math
- Social Studies
- Science
- Special Classes (Music, Art, Spanish, etc.)
- Physical Education
- Therapy/Resource Classes (if appropriate)

Additionally, you child will need to focus on the following as part of their daily school work and you will probably see them come through as homework at some point.

- Spelling Words,
- Reading Vocabulary Words,
- Social Studies Vocabulary Words,

- Science Vocabulary Words (large volume of material and many varied concepts), and
- Science Experiments (you child may not have time to do these at school or process what was done).

Once you've determined your child's curriculum, you'll want to try out many of the activities (either through your own purchases, online games and activities, feedback from your child's teacher, testing results, or activities shown in this book). This experimentation will allow you to determine the activities that your child is good at and tends to enjoy as opposed to those activities with which they have more difficulty.

Exercise Good Judgment

If you discover that you child cannot do many of the activities listed for their grade level, don't panic. Look back at the previous grade level (or several grade levels) and try to determine what skills were taught that led up to that specific ability. For example, if your child can't multiply, you might need to review skip counting, 2, 4, 6, 8…, for example.

Please bear in mind that, in order for your child to pass to the next grade level, Reading, Language Arts and Math are the critical subjects and that Science and Social Studies will not be used to fail your child. Also, your child's year-end testing results will be looked at, along with their school grades, to determine their ability to advance to the next grade.

Emphasize the Most Important

After determining what your child needs to work on, put together a general list to guide you such as the ones that follow. You can copy information found on the internet in order to create your document.

I cannot stress how important it is to specifically address your child's specific needs as opposed to using a ready-made formula. You don't want to waste a lot of time on what your child has already learned. You want to focus you and your child's extremely valuable time on what is specifically required.

> The **clear**er your **goals** are, the more **focused and efficient** you'll be when **teaching your child**.

RELATION WORDS GOALS

- Understands words like above, below, on, under, in, behind, in front of, out of, between, top, bottom, left, right, inside and outside.
- Identifies relationship between objects (before, after, between, near, left, right, inside, outside and close to
- Uses terms such as bigger, smaller, nearer, farther, to express size and distance.

- Greater than, less than, equal to
- Determines equivalence (using physical models) by establishing one-to-one correspondence between two sets (same as, fewer than, and more than).
- Uses the terms all, some and none.
- Describes locatin of various objects in the environment (near, far, up, down, under, back, front, there, above, below)

ADDITION AND SUBTRACTION

- Adds two and three single digit whole numbers presented vertically and horizontally (rewrite vertically) without regrouping.
- Uses models such as base ten blocks, pictorial representation, and number line to explore adding and subtracting two-digit numbers without regrouping.
- Adds and subtracts two-digit whole numbers without regrouping vertically and horizontally (rewrite vertically).
- Uses appropriate mathematical symbols (+, -, =)
- Uses concrete objects to explore the commutative property of addition.
- Explores the property of zero in addition and subtraction.
- Determines addition and subtraction facts up to 18 using strategies such as counting all of a set, part-whole, counting on, counting back, counting up, doubles, property of zero and commutativity of addition.

- Relates addition and subtraction to words, pictures, and concrete models, particularly sums and multiples of ten.
- Recalls addition facts (sums to 18) and related subtraction facts presented vertically and horizontally (rewrite vertically).
- Round whole number to nearest ten.
- Use a variety of methods and tools to compute, including objects, mental computation, and paper and pencils.
- Models, acts out, or uses pictures to solve simple problems.
- Explores one-step word problems related to all appropriate kindergarten objectives.
- Solves one and two-step word problems related to appropriate first-grade objectives. Includes oral and written problems with extraneous information, as well as information from sources such as bar graphs and pictographs.

BAR GRAPHS AND PICTOGRAPHS	
• Constructs and interprets graphs using actual objects or pictorial representations. • Interprets data by reading bar graphs and pictographs using whole unit data.	• Constructs simple graphs using concrete objects such as blocks and squares. • Constructs and uses simple charts, bar, line and circle graphs.
MONEY GOALS	
• Recognizes coins and bills as representing a system of exchange. • Names and identifies values of coins (penny, nickel, dime, quarter) and dollar bills.	• Determines the value of a set of coins up to $0.50 using quarters, nickels, pennies and dimes. • Determines equivalent values of coins up to $0.50.
MEASUREMENT GOALS	
• Compares and describes distances (nearer, farther, and closer to) • Compares and describes lengths (longer than, longest, shorter than, shortest and same length as) • Places objects in order according to size (based on capacity, weight, length, or height) • Understands take less than, more time than • Identifies days, weeks, and months on a calendar. • Selects appropriate units (minutes, hours, days, weeks and months) and appropriate instruments (clocks and calendars) to measure time. • Tells time to the half-hour and hour. • Use a variety of tools to measure. • Compares and weighs real objects using nonstandard measures.	• Explore capacities of containers by pouring and describes capacity in terms of more than, less than, least and most. • Measures with multiple copies of the units of the same size, such as paper clips laid end to end. • Describes, orders, measures length using inches and centimeters. • Selects appropriate instrument for determining specified measurement of height, weight, capacity and temperature. • Compare weight of two real objects (heavier than, lighter than) and capacity of two real containers (more than, less than) using both dry and liquid measure units and compares the height of two real objects (shorter than, taller than)

SHAPES & SIZES GOALS

- Recognize geometric shapes and structures in the environment and specify their location.
- Identifies circle, square, triangle, oval, diamond, rhombus and rectangle in various orientations/positions.
- Identifies spheres, cubes and cones.
- Compares or orders shapes by size (same size as, larger than, smaller than, largest or smallest)

- Can distinguish between geometric shapes, irregular shapes, and shapes with symmetry
- Determines figures are symetrical by folding
- Identifies the shapes (eg, two triangles to make a rectangle) that can be put together to make a given shape.
- Identifies larger than, largest, smaller than, smallest, same size as, same shape as, inside, outside, on, left, right

SOCIAL STUDIES - PERSONAL RESPONSIBILITY

- Accepts and carries out assigned tasks.
- Demonstrates responsibility for one's actions.
- Arranges personal experiences in sequence.
- Places related events in chronological order.
- Sequences terms which denote time.
- Uses calendar to find special days.
- Participates in a group as a follower or leader
- Knows Pledge of Allegiance
- Identify symbols of our country like Uncle Sam, the bald eagle, flag and the Statue of Liberty.
- Describe patriotic holidays – MLK, Mem. Day, Vets Day, Columbus Day, Flag Day
- Look at flags from different countries.

- Uses the following location words – near, over, far, up, down, under, back, front, here, there, left and right
- Uses a calendar. Acquires information through observing and listening.
- Organizes information in a meaningful way.
- Arranges events, facts and ideas in sequence.
- Identify past, present and future.
- Develops the ability to acquire information through interpreting graphs and charts.
- Recalls and tells major ideas following a listening activity.
- Acquires information through reading, observing and listening.
- Arranges, events, facts and ideas in sequence.
- Explains why certain words, pictures or ideas are grouped together.
- Recognizes and states a problem related to appropriate activities.

SOCIAL STUDIES - CONFLICT RESOLUTION

- Identifies and states problems related to a personal experience.
- Communicates several ways to solve problems.
- Identifies best sources to answer questions to solve problems.
- Chooses appropriate solutions to solve problems.

- Makes decisions and identifies the consequence of choice Follows established rules
- Shows respect toward others
- Works within a group, following set rules of procedures to complete an assigned tasks.
- Identifies and uses alternative methods of conflict resolution.

SOCIAL STUDIES - PEOPLE GOALS

- States ways in which people are alike and different.
- Identifies the President as the leader of our country.
- Describes how children and families use resources to meet basic needs and wants in different climates.
- Recognizes that different cultural groups have different characteristics.

- Recognizes that people live in different places for different reasons (jobs, families).
- Names and describes the roles of community helpers who produce goods and/or services including firefighters, police officers, doctors, dentists, bus drivers and farmers.
- Recognizes that some of our goods come from foreign countries.

SOCIAL STUDIES - MAPS & MACHINES GOALS

- Determines that some toys are small scale models of real objects.
- Tells whether a statement is true or make-believe.
- Compares modes of land, air and water transportation and how goods are transported.
- Map – recognizes characteristics like hills, mountains, continents, and islands as land forms; lakes, oceans and rivers as bodies of water.
- Identifies pictorial symbols of maps.
- Uses a simple map to identify North, South, East and West.
- Names and locales one's state, country and continent on a map and a globe.

- Reads simple picture maps.
- Identifies a map as a drawing of a particular location (classroom, neighborhood)
- Describes purpose of a map key.
- Compares and contrasts globe and world map.
- Identifies compass rose as directional tool.
- Describes diff. between natural resources (water, soil, wood, coal, etc.) and human resources (people at work)
- Explains that a map is a drawing of a particular location, e.g., classroom, neighborhood.

SCIENCE GOALS

- Take care of plants and animals.
- Recognize different seasons.
- Understanding of nutrition, exercise and healthy living.
- Safety procedures for home, school, outdoors, playground, vehicles, bicycles, etc.
- Observe, compare, classify, measure, pedict, hypothesize and infer
- Explore scientific equipment and materials.
- Describes states of matter.
- Understand simple machines, magnets and electricity.
- Perform activities related to each (rocks, soil, air) and sky (clouds, sun, moon, stars)

PHYSICAL SKILLS GOALS

FINE MOTOR
- Draw
- Cut with scissors
- Write name

GROSS MOTOR
- Walk backward
- Ball Games
- Sports skills
- Social Games
- Attempts a somersault
- Bounces ball two times and then catches it.
- Cathches playground ball with two hands.
- Gallops forward
- Hops on one foot at a time
- Hops on preferred foot for a distance
- Jumps forward a distance of 10"
- Jumps forward and backward
- Jumps from bottom step to floor
- Jumps over a small object
- Jumps up 8-10"
- Kicks a large ball that is rolling
- Kicks a stationery ball
- Pumps swing to maintain motion
- Pushes and pulls a wagon
- Runs a distance of 10' avoiding obstacles
- Runs on tiptoes
- Skips 5-10 seconds
- Swimming
- Throws a playground ball 5-7'.
- Throws a playground ball underhand to an adult.

CREATIVE DEVELOPMENT GOALS

- Exposure to variety of art, music, literature and drama
- Share what learn through drawings, constructions, discussions, making charts, etc.
- Using objects as symbols for other items
- Engage freely in dramatic play

ADAPTIVE SKILLS GOALS

- Zipping
- Putting on shoes
- Washing hands
- Buttoning
- Eating with spoon and fork
- Putting materials/belongings away

Enquiry Schedule

All right, you know what your child needs to study and you've got a pretty good feel for the activities that your child likes and dislikes.

Now, you're going to create a daily schedule, based on the time you have available, to which to hold yourself (and your child) accountable each day. The following example was used as a home school schedule for a younger (early elementary-aged) child.

Jack's Homeschool Schedule

Time	Subject	Monday	Tuesday	Wednesday	Thursday	Friday
7:20 a.m.	Vocabulary & Reading	●	●	●	●	
8:00 a.m.	Math	●	●	●	●	
8:50 a.m.	Break if Work Done	X	●			
9:00 a.m.	Language Arts	●	●	●	●	
10:00 a.m.	Snack & Recess	●	●	●	●	
10:30 a.m.	Writing & Cursive	●	●	●		
11:15 a.m.	Science	●	●	●		
12:00 p.m.	Lunch	●	●	●		
12:30 p.m.	Social Studies			●		
1:30 p.m.	Specials	Music	Art	PE	Spanish	Health

Adjust the schedule to the age and needs of your child and, if you find that your schedule rarely changes, you may want to laminate it so that it is reusable week after week. Instead of stickers, simply checking off each subject with a dry erase marker may serve as an incentive for a student to stay focused. Post the schedule when it is regularly seen in passing by all members of the household and it can serve as a reward for working done during the week. Mar a box on the schedule with an "x" or fill it in as a black box and public posting may serve as a deterrent to a child's choosing not to do a lesson one day.

Build in breaks dependent upon the age of your child. One of our all-time favorites has been to take a restroom break and then bounce a balloon until it hits the floor (which signifies that break time is over). Other options may be to toss a basketball, take a scooter break in the garage or any type of physical movement. See the chapter that deals with behavior in this book for more ideas.

IV. Birth of Brilliance

Lucky baby, born into a family filled with love and tenderness. Mommy promises to be one of the best. Daddy chases away the dark concerns of the world. Your baby's first few months are a misty cloud of soft kisses, close and gentle touches, and all the warmth and comfort that is mother. Relief that the pregnancy has been cleared, exhaustion from the ordeal, concern over the new baby's care, and the many sleepless nights are softened and forgotten in time and are replaced with magnificent new memories filled with wonder and charm.

This chapter goes over what your child will be learning in the coming years, prerequisites to academic learning, early childhood, basic life and conversational skills, and establishing a basic household schedule and chores for your child. The need for these skills is hard to imagine when you're holding a delicate newborn; but quick to come into needful action.

Things to Come

Learning to Speak	Acting Out/Saying new vocabulary verbs
	Acting out play scenarios using toys, tools and other available resources
	Listening to/Creating music CDs
	Watching/Creating DVDs
	Learning/Singing songs
	Learning/Reciting rhymes and poems
	Learning phonics for reading
	Matching pictures to real life objects
	Naming toys and parts of things
Using Your Hands	Push, pull, twist, pour, tear, spoon, tong, tie, button, zip, snap, clothes pin, etc.
	Computer mouse
	Imitate lines, circles, shapes
	Draw
	Cut with scissors
	Write letters and sentences (as child is learning phonics)
	Learn to type (summer months)
Using Your Body	Push up on forearms from tummy, roll over backwards and forwards, pull up to standing, sit up, crawl, stand, walk, run, hop, jump, kick, climb, tiptoe, gallop, skip
	Push/Pull, carry, hit, throw, catch

Jeanne Mifflin

Reading	Restaurant and trade logos
	Consonant sounds
	Vowels and most common sounds
	Simple rhyming words – cat, bat, hat
	Sight words (ongoing)
	Combined consonants – ch, th, sh
	Vowel sounds and combinations
	Listening to Your New Reader Read for 20 Minutes a Day
	Comprehension (ongoing)
	Grammar
Math	Counting, skip counting, place counting
	Addition, subtraction, multiplication, division
	Fractions, geometry, decimals, probability and statistics, measurement, word problems
Social Studies	Community – fireman, policeman, teachers, post office, etc.
	Ancient civilizations
	American history
	World history and cultures
	Economics and government
Science	Universe & Planets (emphasis on Earth)
	Living and Nonliving things
	Machines
	Scientific method and scientists

Tips for Six Months to a Year

Ample resources are available in the form of quality books and online resources that will lead you through many of the basic skills that your baby needs to acquire. A creative curriculum book for infants is even available. The following tips and tricks may serve in troubleshooting difficulties you run into unexpectedly.

Sitting

To help your child learn to sit, place soft pillows in the "v" of a corner with a pillow behind his back (as shown in photo). Prop your child against the pillow learning slightly backward and place toys in front of him that he can attempt to reach and play with, thereby gaining strength in his abdominal muscles.

Strengthen Legs

Very gently push against his legs to help make them stronger or gently test to see if you can build up his leg muscles by testing his stance for a little bit every day.

Pull Up to Standing

Enlist the aid of a helper for this exercise. When your baby can sit upright, by himself, in his crib and has acquired some strength in his legs, have your helper stand your baby up, close to the rail, and then you gently place his hands on the rail briefly. Your helper gently lowers your baby back down into a sitting position in the crib.

Encourage your baby to try (to lift himself up by holding onto the rail) by hiding beneath his eye level outside of the crib and, then, raising your hands up and placing them on the rail, follow this by pulling yourself up. Stay at it for several weeks. Expect this to turn into a fun game for all of you. Keep up the enthusiasm for the task by applauding and cheering as your baby gets closer and closer.

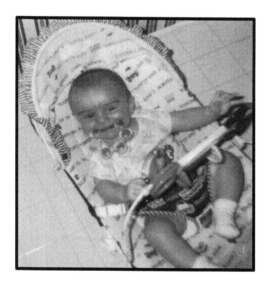

Achieving Brilliance at Home

Roll Backwards

You will know that your baby is getting ready to roll over if they are playing with their feet a lot and seem to be getting stronger. With your baby on his tummy, shake a rattle or musical toy just behind baby's shoulder to see if you can get him to roll over.

Roll Forward

Once your baby has gained strength in his legs, arms, back and stomach, he will be able to roll over. That's why it's so important that you child have some significant tummy time every day. If your child screams, use the TV to achieve partially diverted attention to distract him from his discomfort. Just make sure that the show you've selected is one for which *he* seems to have a keen interest.

Yes/No

Offer something they like, shake your head and say,"Yes." Then, let them has a taste as you are repeating the word, "Yes." Make a frowny face and offer them something you know they don't like (like a taste of pickle) as you're shaking your head and saying, "No." Repeat daily until yes and no become a part of their daily language.

Legs

Start holding them up and gently testing whether they are ready to try and stand. Just as with starting any other exercise program, start out slowly and build up.

Language

Sing the same lullabies over and over and over. Say, "mama," and, "daddy" for as long as it takes.

Crawling

For learning to push up on their arms from their tummy, place a TV high up across the floor and put on a kids show in which your baby seems to be particularly interested. See if they won't practice a little bit every day to lift up in order to see the TV show. It is important that your child learn to crawl and they may not do so unless motivated in some way. Don't waste their precious their developmental time.

Once your child is starting to crawl a bit and has confidence in it, you will want to put him in ball pits and let him try to crawl out to gain strength. This is also the time to place him in a pile of leaves in the back yard to see whether he can free himself. If he's crying, take him out. If he is hesitant only, leave him in the leaves in order that he may test out his limits for himself.

When they are up on all fours and you want to motivate them to starting trying to crawl, put them in a kid's tunnel set a little way in (especially at the playground) and see if they will try to crawl out.

Solid Food

If your baby balks at starting solid food like cereal, wait a couple of weeks and try again.

Sleeping Through the Night

Lots of exhausting activity (even crying), a good dinner, a warm bath, a good book, and a soft warm mommy in a rocking chair done in the same way, at the same time, every night, will generally lull your baby to sleep after an initial period of adjustment. Every night, just try to get a little closer to your goal. Be sure and exhaust your baby, but not yourself, just before bedtime or you'll be too tired to put the baby to bed. Learning to pace yourself is a big part of motherhood.

If your child continues to have trouble sleeping through the night, see if there is a problem like a neighbor's barking dog, a night shift daddy sneaking in to kiss him goodnight, or a brother or sister that wants to "play" with the baby at night.

Learn to accept that crying is a natural part of everyday life with children. It's actually a great exercise for them (assuming all of their physical and emotional needs have been cared for and the crying is just part of learning how to put himself back to sleep).

Tricks for One to Three Year Olds

If at all possible, inside your house, set up a room with a small children's slide, a tunnel, a fabric playhouse filled with plastic balls set up as a ball pit, and a small trampoline with a handle that your child can grasp in order to learn to jump (after he has mastered walking).

Stairs

First, you will teach your child how to go up and down stairs in an all fours position. Make sure they go up facing the stairs and teach them to come down in reverse, but still facing the stairs. As they become more agile, they can come down facing away from the stairs (but holding onto the rail).

The best way to learn stairs in on your indoor child's exercise room slide steps. Just make sure you place exercise mats against the walls in case your child slips.

When your baby is fully mobile is the time when you will want to start working with them at public restaurant play places.

Warning: If your child is hesitant to try out the play areas and just wants to sit instead of playing, you need to prepared to go in and out of the structures with your child and guide their little arms and legs as to how they should move them. Be gently firm and encouraging..

Walking

Children pretty much learn to walk in the following pattern -- pull up, stand, begin to move around room holding on to something, begin to walk from object to object that they can grab on to, able to walk a few steps without holding on, and will then (especially, if you walk them around the house or playground daily) begin to walk more and more on their own. Please not that your child will fall a lot which is why I favor a designated and padded indoor child's exercise room (if you have the space for it).

Using Hands

Pinching, pushing, pulling, spinning, banging two things together, putting in and taking out of containers, putting tops on and taking tops off of containers, letting go of toys, trying to scribble with a fatty crayon, and finger painting with food are some of the first activities your will do with your child in order to help them learn to use their hands and fingers. Encourage your child to hold their own bottle, when they're a baby, and buy them a cute spoon (that *they* like) and encourage them to try and feed themselves sooner rather than later.

Imitation

Try to get your child to imitate you. For example, if you want to teach your child how to clap their hands, say "Yea!" at an appropriate time when playing a game and clap your hands (while your child is looking at you). Do it again several times. If your child does not respond, say, "Yeah," and gently placed your hands over their hands and clap their hands for them. Practice every day (for several weeks, if necessary) until your child learns to clap their hands on their own and when it's appropriate to clap hands.. It's a big thrill the day they finally do it the right way and at the right time!

Language - One and a Half

Once your child is a year and a half old, you will want to start with the following songs and rhymes. You will provide lots of repetition of 2-5 rhymes until they actually know them. "Old McDonald" sung very slowly and low (but high-pitched for the parts that change), clapping only in order to teach patty cake, clapping hands in excitement, and peek a boo hands are just a few of the skills you will work on with your child.

Achieving Brilliance at Home

Twinkle, Twinkle, Little Star

Twinkle, twinkle, little star *(hold hands up and open and close fingers in a blinking motion)*

How I wonder what you are. *(continue blinking fists)*

Up above the world so high *(blinking fists continue up in the air over your head)*

Like a diamond in the sky *(make diamond shape with your fingers and look through it to spy your child)*

Twinkle, twinkle, little star *(hold hands up and open and close blinking fingers)*

How I wonder what you are. *(continue blinking fists until ends)*

Sit in front of a floor length mirror with your child on your lap and walk their little hands through the above motions. Do not worry about their fingers, just try to gently guide their arms and hands through the motions. Then say, "You try,". Don't be surprised if they can't do it. Keep doing that a couple of times a day for several weeks (rewarding them with a snippet of a treat afterward if they try) and you'll be thrilled when they actually start trying to do it.

For a bedtime story, as an additional activity, get a book or toy that contains this rhyme and point to the appropriate picture as you say the words while your child is sitting on your lap.

The following are the first songs and rhymes your child is likely to learn. Try to have two books – one songbook and CD that shows the hand movements you're supposed to make and provides you with the tune and the words, and also an illustrated storybook that shows pictures of the words that you are singing. Always sing the song attached to a specific theme. You will introduce a new theme or lesson about every two weeks to a month and can start when you're baby is about one and a half (although you are just trying to get their attention mainly at this point).

- "If You're Happy and You Know It" (Theme: Me)
- "Head and Shoulders, Knees and Toes" (Theme: Me)
- "Itsy Bitsy Spider" (Theme: Farm Animals or Home)
- "Jingle Bells" (Theme: Christmas)
- "Hickory, Dickory, Dock" -- when you child starts learning to count, you will "bong" the number of counts after you say the number word. (Theme: Home)
- "Monkeys Jumping on the Bed" (Theme: Wild Animals or Home) This song is especially useful when your child is learning to jump. If you don't have a mini-trampoline with a handle, have your child hold your hands as they jump on a mattress or sofa cushion. Don't try to jump yourself unless you are athletic.
- "Jack and Jill" (Theme: Nursery Rhymes)
- "Old McDonald" (Theme: Farm Animals)
- "A-B-C Song" -- never sing this song without pointing to the appropriate letter of the alphabet. (Theme: Letters)
- Make up or locate a song on CD for the days of the week. Place a large children's calendar low on a wall and always point to the days of the week as you sing them. Make up silly or useful names to help reinforce the idea of time during the week. For example, if you child goes to karate practice on Tuesday and Thursday nights, you will say " karate Tuesday" and "kick-it Thursday." You might say something like "Funday Monday," (if appropriate) 'T-Shirt Tuesday," or "Wacky Wednesday." Ideally,.you will take a representational picture of your child to use in making the day headings on their calendar.

- Sing the months of the year to "Silent Night" and end with, "twelve months in a year," sung twice. Always point to a symbol for that month on the child's calendar. For example, the following symbols are traditionally associated with each month – January (snowman), February (hearts), March (wind, lion, lamb), April (rain showers), May (flowers), June (boats or swimming pool), July (fireworks), August (sun), September (school), October (fall), November (turkey), and December (Holy Family, star or Santa Claus)).
- "Rain, Rain, Go Away" (Theme: Home or Weather)
- "Ring Around the Rosy" (Theme: Gardening, Home or Me)

Eating Problems

Many children start to have eating difficulties during the toddler years because of self-imposed food limitations. If you child prefers smooth consistencies, you may want to make a "goodnight pudding" in the blender that contains a vitamin, yogurt, peanut butter (if your child does not have an allergic sensitivity), banana and anything else you would like to include that won't significantly alter the texture or flavor.

Potty Training

The typical routine is to sit your child on the potty and read them a children's storybook written especially for toilet training. I think this works even better if you can find a stuffed animal or character that is close to the one featured in the book. Additionally, a DVD showing children happily learning to go potty is appropriate and you may even want your child to sit on the potty (in the middle of the living room) during the period in which they watch the video. A treat, such as a cookie, is appropriate at the close of the potty session.

Alternatively, there is a classic book on the market that touts potty training in less than a day that I used and still believe to be the best on the market. The way I followed the book was to (1) select an official day to train (and I followed the specific instructions in the book), (2) have my child teach a doll to "go potty," and (3) never put my child in diapers again.

An additional step you may need to take, that is not outlined in the book, is to purchase an engaging plastic toilet seat (like those with cute fish inside) to carry in a large beach bag when you are out for the day. Practice a lot with the seat at home and, then, practice when you go to stores and restaurants. It's very strange, I know, but it will help your child learn to feel comfortable going potty everywhere. As time passes, start phasing out the seat. Keep your potty purchase receipt in the side pocket of your beach bag to cover you in the unlikely event that you encounter difficulty with a store's security personnel.

Techniques for Three to Seven Year Olds

Teach your child the give and take ping-pong of conversation earlier rather than later. The following ideas will help you learn to teach your child specific skills.

Early Reading & Writing Ideas

Point to objects on the cover of a book and point to words (even before your child reads) so they can get the idea that *you are reading* the words. After you've read the story, summarize it in three, five-word, sentences and have your child repeat then back, one sentence at a time. You may also want to act out the story if your child is having a hard time understanding it.

Copy (color copies preferable) the pages of a fairytale or storybook that you child is familiar with and cut them out to use for story sequencing activities. Model telling the story with the pictures. First match the picture to the page and say, "Bobby got dirty," (point to the dirt on Bobby in the picture). "Bobby had a bath," (point to Bobby in the tub and say "bath" again). Do this for all five pictures. Do this every day (for as long as it takes) using the same story and pictures until your child starts to respond by telling the story himself verbally and holding up the correct picture in the correct order. Use only three to five pictures for the first few books. Be sure to point to the boy each time you say, "Bobby."

Using the copies you made previously, affix hook and loop tape to the back and use them to act out the story on a felt board using words like "next, then, finally," etc. Have fun seeing how far your child can go before they stumble on their words.

When you are teaching your child to read or write, put most of your emphasis on the lower case letters as those are used the most. Make a game of matching upper and lower case letters (starting with five sets at a time) by writing the corresponding letters on little squares of cardstock. If your child is having difficulty, you may want to color code the cards at first. Mix in easier letters to match with more difficult letters to match so that your child does not become frustrated. As part of this exercise, review with your child the sound that each letter makes. www.starfall.com has great videos for learning to read.

You will have to be creative in coming up with little zooms, bumps, hills, and valleys or whatever to teach your student how to make their letters. Base your instructional words around a theme or hobby your child likes. For example, you might want to say "hop, jump, roll," for a child who loves the playground or "skip, curtsey, cartwheel" for a girl who loves movement. Most kids like to learn how to write their names first. You may want to create your own dry erase sheet that is reusable or make copies of a worksheet you have created yourself.

To teach your child to read, you will need to teach them sight words (locate "Dolch" word lists online) and make sure you are looking at the words for your child's grade or reading level) and phonics. See if you can find a good used reading instruction textbook for teachers on amazon.com as the books available for parents tend to be rather dry. The library is a wealth of valuable guidance and information as regards teaching your child to read. Some children's television shows also have web sites with reading guidance.

Buy (or make) a set of cards that show the letter, of the sound they are learning, on the front and a picture with the word written on it on the back. Make up a song along the lines of "a goes ă like apple…" Flip the card and point to the "a" in the word, "apple." Sing the phrase (Try "Farmer in the Dell") and put the letter card through a slit into a box for added fun.

Practice writing every day. Write on a dry erase board or purchased dry erase workbook.

If they can read and write, have them start writing short stories.

Give them a children's encyclopedia or picture book to give them ideas. If they are not ready to start writing stories, just keep storytelling together and have them write three-letter words into a story (or drawings woven into a story).

Early Math Ideas

Sing the twelve months of the year to the tune of "Silent Night" and end with "twelve months in a year" sang twice. Point to the month symbols on a calendar or use month symbol cutouts and have your child place the appropriate cutout in the correct position on a felt board as you sing the song.

Using a box with a slit cut into the top, have your child count poker chips to a number you specify as they push them through the slot into the box. Count with your child as they take them out of the box. Use with a worksheet if desired.

Gather two sets of items -- for example, one plastic toy kitchen dish set and one set of plastic animals. Mix them all together and then have your child describe an item, tell what it's used for, and then sort it by a specified attribute such as color, type of object, etc. In the case of large items (such as a stove, refrigerator, sink, etc.), copy and cut apart pictures so that your student can sort them that way.

Using a stuffed animal dog, sing "Where Oh Where Has My Little Dog Gone?" and then have your child find the dog. Describe exactly where the dog can be found. For example, the dog is UNDER the table, ON TOP of the table, BEHIND the chair, etc.. You may want to read *Go Dog Go* as part of the fun.

Science Ideas

Teach the seven continents using a spinning globe (yes, you may go through several) and the following piggyback song using "Old McDonald" as the tune:

Jeanne Mifflin

> There are seven continents all over the world.
> Antarctica, Australia, Africa and Asia,
> North America, South America and Europe,
> There are seven continents all over the world.

Your child will point to each continent and gleefully spin the globe, as you hold it steady, to point to each continent.

- Use the song, "My Bonnie Lies Over the Ocean," to sing the names of the oceans.

> My Bonnie lies over the ocean,
> My Bonnie lies over the sea
>
> My Bonnie lies over the ocean,
> Oh, bring back my Bonnie to me.
>
> Arctic, Atlantic, Pacific and Indian too, (repeat)
> Arctic, Atlantic, Pacific and Indian too;
>
> And some people say there's a Southern Ocean!
> (said as an aside)

To stress the importance of hand washing, use the following rhyme:

> Germs are little monsters that make me sick,
> That I can't see 'em is their trick,
> But I can keep them outside of me,
> If I wash my hands before I eat.

Social Studies Ideas

- Teach your child a song wherein they sing their full name, street address and phone number (planet and solar system, if appropriate). Some children's CDs have songs like this already worked out that you can use.
- Social Skills: If possible, take digital pictures of your child

displaying different actions and emotions and turn them into a series of sequencing cards that show the expected outcome of different actions. For example, have a card with your child having a tantrum, a card of your child in time-out, and a card with something like, "Find toy, play happy," depicted on it. Use these cards to walk your child through whatever steps you choose to lead them out of a tantrum or other undesirable behavior.

Sample Theme Lesson Trees

Earlier in this book, I led your through creating Green Lesson Trees. The following examples show you exactly how to create lesson trees for early skills training.

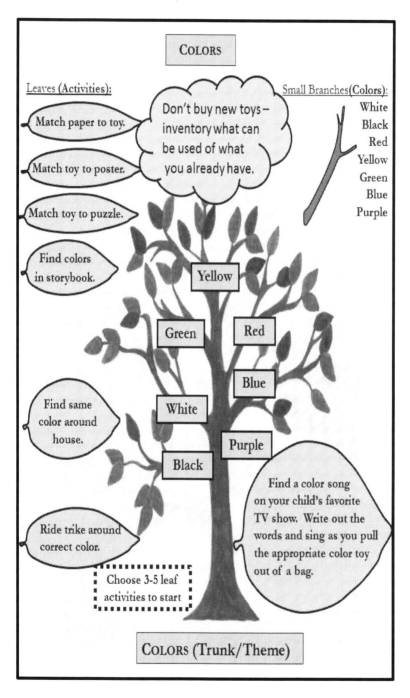

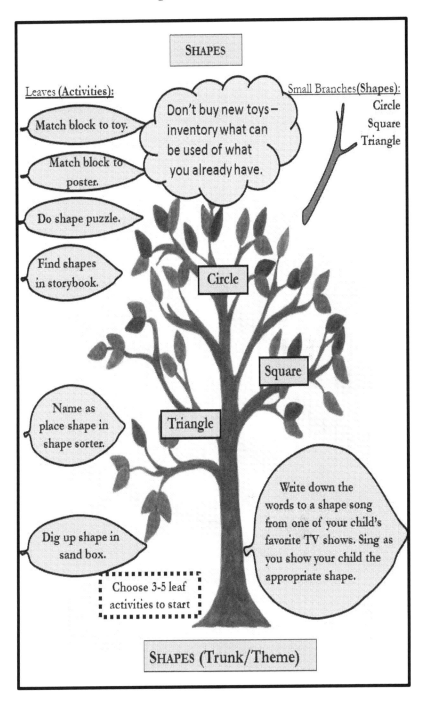

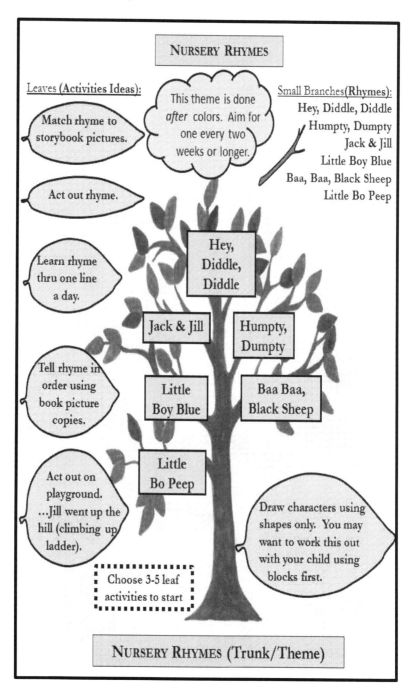

Time Management

- Never leave you child with nothing to do "while you get ready." Always have an instructional video, educational computer game, book to read, or something else to do while waiting.

- Use cue words to let your child know when to react immediately. Always plan for the next activity to help motivate your child through. For example, instead of saying, "Put your shoes on," say, "'Put your shoes on so we can go to the doctor's office, to the park, to the grocery store and, then, when we get home, we'll have ice cream." Plan things they like into your plans if at all possible to help buy compliance (sorry, but a mom get exhausted). Give only two directions to start when your child is very young.

Daily Living Skills

Go ahead and start teaching your child opposites. Use a poster or flash cards that show appropriate pictures. Some of the most important opposites your child will need to know are "give me/take," and "same/different."

Plan out several activities for each opposite set, using the Green Lesson Tree format, for practice. Feel free to enlarge the lesson trees if you're having trouble reading the print. No need to come up with a form. Roughly plan out your tree and write the activities on construction paper "leaves" to serve as a quick reference as you're working with your child.

Long before you sit down to officially "teach" your child a "lesson," you will need to teach them myriad daily living skills such as the following. I've provided a lesson tree for one of these skills to show you how to adapt a lesson tree for a single purpose.

Jeanne Mifflin

Sitting at the Table

(See Green Lesson Tree next page for "Sitting at the Table.")

The following discusses how to teach your child to eat with a spoon or hold a crayon while sitting at a child's table. If your child has not reached this point, please teach the "Sitting at the Table" lesson tree found on the next page *first*.

1. Call your child to the table.
2. Guide his hands to pull the chair out.
3. Nudge his body into the chair.
4. Push his chair in for him or teach him to lift the chair and walk forward closer to the table.
5. Guide his hand (with your hand on top) as to how to use the spoon. Look at how you hold a spoon and position his fingers accordingly. Then, guide his hand to pick up some food and carry it to his mouth. For a crayon, position his fingers and then place your hand over his to color (gently please).
6. Physically block his ability to leave the table. You may want to place a child's table against a wall so you can sit on the floor next to the table and still block his leaving with your knee.
7. Use a cue phrase like "learning time" or "time to eat:" to signal your child that it's time to come to the table. If you've got good food or fun materials waiting for him, he will learn that meals and learning time are fun and will begin to come willingly – even looking forward to it.

Follow the same procedure for teaching your child other skills like holding a glass or cup, dressing and undressing and how to brush their teeth. If you can create a song, to make it more fun, your child will learn faster. Simply sing-song the words if you feel you have no talent for song or rhyme.

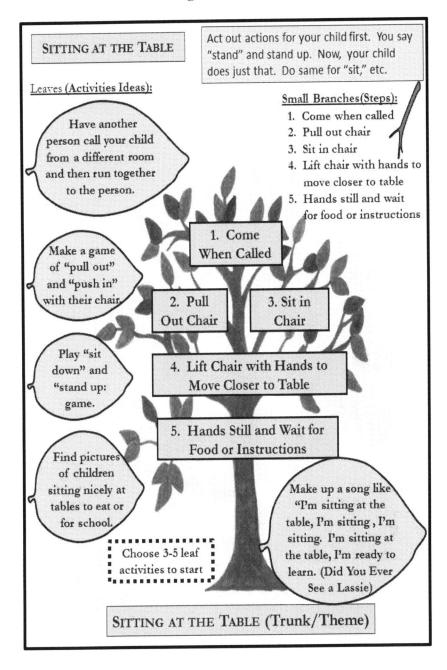

Other Daily Living Skills

Important skills that you will need to teach your preschooler include those that follow. Practice creating your own lesson trees to teach the following as these lessons are very important starting points.

- **Emergency Preparedness:** Where to go and what to do in an emergency like a fire, tornado, or if you become lost. The Federal Emergency Management Agency (FEMA) has a free coloring book that you can order online. There are also children's DVDs available on this subject.

- **Daily Hygiene Skills:** There is a great series of preschool videos available online that model daily living skills and Montessori exercises for skill building. Search for "Preschool Power." Teeth brushing videos can be found at your dentist's web site or on YouTube. Just make sure you locate a video *before* you intend to show it to your child. That way, you can avoid any unexpected surprises.

- **Chores:** www.handipoints.com has great online interactive charts on which your child can track their chores. Just make sure you create a lesson tree for the chores you want to teach. Take a picture of the completed chore (when possible) to show your child the standard when Mom does the chore and to which you hope they will aspire. Break the chore down into specific steps and teach each step (three to five at a time). Create a Green Lesson Tree for all chores in the beginning until you have a good sense of the rate at which your child learns.

- **Play Skills:** Teach your child how to play with his toys and the purpose for which they are used in real life. You will then want him to practice playing with his toys, the right way, on his own. Resources are plentiful on the internet on this issue.

Achieving Brilliance at Home

In the beginning, it may be difficult to overcome your sense of personal dignity as you roll around on the floor playing with your child. If it feels embarrassing, you're probably on the right track.

As a general rule, the sillier and more playful you are as you teach your child, the faster and easier it will be for them to learn. Go ahead – have fun! No one's watching.

> **The sillier and more playful you are,
> The easier it will be for your child to learn.**

V. Animation of Brilliance

One of the very worse things that can happen to you, as a parent, is to discipline your child for misbehavior only to find out that they have an ear infection or other illness. If you ever notice that your child unexpectedly begins to tantrum, whine, complain and fuss (more than usual), the first course of action is to rule out illness and the second is to make sure that they have an outlet for all that kid energy.

Make sure you have plenty of physical exertion built into your day or you may mistake venting of pent up energy for defiance. Normally, a child who has fallen into a routine will become comfortable with it and stop fighting after a week or so. If you child suddenly revolts, (1) have them checked at the doctor, (2) make sure they have outlets for their physical energy, and (3) switch out your materials.

If your child has grown bored of the materials you're using with him, matching them to the seasons, holidays or his special interests will restore the novelty. For this reason, I suggest that, unless your child is still doing very well with and still enjoying a particular set of materials, you switch out materials by month to keep them fresh.

Be aware that sometimes your child might try to antagonize you to disrupt the learning period. Try to remain calm no matter the provocation. Some children will even try to antagonize a sibling to try and get the sibling to tantrum in order to disrupt a learning period. Watch for this type of pattern if you're teaching more than one child at a time.

Teach Them Now
or
Take Care of Them Later

Special Thoughts

1. What special resources does my family have that I can use to teach my child – library, swimming pool, close family, lots of toys, siblings, nearby park, museum close by, etc.

2. What is my child particularly good at?

3. What does my child have the most trouble with?

4. What do I think is the greatest risk to my child's future and will them help them somewhat overcome or better cope with this danger?

What <u>exactly</u> do I want my child to learn? (Curriculum)

I promise to look over or prepare my materials in advance. I will:

- Show them how I do it using prepared toys, games and other activities,

- Help them do it several times,
- Let them practice doing it the way I showed them,
- See if they can do it when they are alone, and
- Give them enough practice opportunities to ensure that they experience the feelings of ease and success.

If they are not learning, I will ask myself:

- Do they have the foundation skills needed to learn this new task? In other words, make sure they can add easily before you try to teach them to multiply.
- Is it a work problem or a routine problem.
- Did I use materials or rewards that they like enough to work for or did I use what was on sale?
- Did I teach them what they know are supposed to do and to what standard?
- Did I come up with a checklist to give them a goal to aim for in order to complete this group of tasks.

I will write down their behavior for at least one day and review it for patterns and changes I could make to support their positive responses to my requests.

Is there a main problem that other problems spin off of such as:

- Hunger?
- Time of day?
- Type of work?
- Materials used for teaching?

> **What does my mother's intuition say about the problem?**

If it's a behavior problem, I will:

- Stick to my planned routine,

- Not be caught off guard by fussing, whining and tantruming and I will allow lots of extra time during the first two weeks for these new schedule behaviors,

- Supply promised rewards for good work, along with lots of praise and enthusiasm, the *moment* they begin to behave well (but after they've finished the job), and

- No TV, computer, or whatever happens to be their favorite leisure time activity unless they worked for me through learning.

Secret Behavior Monitoring

The first course of action, if you're truly interested in learning to work with you child, is to determine typical naughty behaviors that you child employs, as well as how you will react when those ploys are utilized.

Over the course of several days, I want you to take a notebook with you, everywhere that you go with your child, and write down whenever they misbehave and how you react to it. Also make note of when the misbehavior is likely to occur. See if you can find any patterns. You will also want to come up with ideas of how you can flip the situation to your advantage.

The following chart provides an example of a typical behavior issue between a mom and her child.

Behavior	Date	Situation	My Reaction
Tantrum	8/15	Refused to get dressed	Frustration, anger, fear -- I started crying; gave up and let him watch TV.

Most of the problems that you have with your child can be easily eliminated through the use of a consistent daily schedule and the momentum of daily routine. Getting started, breaks due to vacation or illness, and breaks from routine due to holiday activities or travel are the times when you will need to reinstate your structure and get your child back on track.

The above problem is most likely to happen (1) if you have not known how to guide your child into a structured routine and are beginning now, (2) there has been a break in routine (as mentioned above), or (3) *you* do not have the self-discipline to impose and maintain a structure yourself. Give yourself a break – introduce some structure into *your* life. Things will go much more smoothly for you and your family if you try.

Regarding the problem at hand, you can flip this situation by scheduling your mornings around your child's favorite TV show (as an idea).

The way this works is that you establish a routine whereby your child must be up and dressed with teeth brushed, hair combed, and breakfast eaten by the time their show comes on at 7:30 a.m. (for example).

Even if they're running late, when they hear the music begin, they will tend to hurry up fast.

Of course, you must enforce not allowing your child to watch the show, even if they tantrum, in the beginning. Once their show is over, the TV goes off immediately.

Behavior	Date	Situation	My Reaction
Tore up coloring page and broke crayon	8/15	Refused to try or let me help him	Gave him a snack and play break so I could cool off

This is a situation where you will need to be a little firmer in order to establish your authority. DO NOT reward your child for this behavior by giving him a snack and a play break.

DO tape the page and the crayon back together and make him sit there for at least 20 minutes. If he refuses, you will need to enforce a consequence. Scary, I know. Consequences will be discussed on the pages that follow.

Gather your "current behavior" information for 3-5 days (if you can) and include weekend and outing behaviors. You may find that your child is so surprised by this strange "writing down" reaction to his behavior that it seems to give you a little reprieve from the colorful histrionics.

The number one problem you will be looking for (as you analyze the patterns of behavior for both you and your child) is situations where **you reinforce his bad behavior by your own actions.** **For example, giving up is a great way to reinforce the very behavior you don't want.** Letting your child watch TV, in addition to your giving up, sets up a **tantrum lifestyle** for you and your child. *Is that really what you're hoping for?* He knows the routine -- as soon as he sees you starting to get frustrated, he'll push harder because he knows that it's the first step toward you giving up and letting him watch TV.

==Look over your list and *plan specific alternative behaviors for yourself.*== You will probably have to carry your list around for a few weeks until you have developed new habits of responding. For example, you can say something like, =="TV and computer time is the same as reading time -- fifteen minutes of reading equals fifteen minutes of TV or computer time."== Yes, they're going to hate this idea. *Expect tantrums.* ==If you're going to have to deal with Rock & Roll tantrums anyway, at least let them happen on your terms.==

As an aside, you may want to set up a "Temper Tantrum Town" in a little nook in your house with a bean bag chair, good behavior posters and books, etc. It may also help you to sing a fun song to yourself to lighten your mood. Although it won't affect your child's tantrum in the slightest, it may really calm you down to sing, **"Let me take you to Temper Tantrum Town; let me take you to Temper Tantrum Town,"** to the tune of **"Funkytown." Funk dancing is required en route** (just make sure that your child is facing away from you).

Structure and Routine

Create a daily schedule and then follow it. You can either plan for a successful experience for both you and your child, or you can plan on dealing with multiple tantrums and much frustration on both sides. Even with excellent planning, it's still going to be rough going at first.

Plan out wake-up and bedtime, breakfast, lunch, dinner, snack breaks, lesson times, and household chores for the week for all family members. Also work in church, Scouting, athletics, clubs, other regular activities, field trips, etc. Don't forget grocery shopping and laundry.

Knowing What to Teach

If at all possible, try to purchase a book or access free online lessons or video activities to create the first few tasks to work on with your child. Creating your own curriculum completely from scratch is a monumental job even for professional teachers.

Selective Reward Ideas

As you're making notes of your child's behavior, also make notes of what they particularly enjoy doing and/or the toys, games, TV shows and foods that they best.

Think through and plan out how you will reward your child for specific desired behaviors. Make certain that you withhold the promised treat or reward if they don't do what you asked of them or your life will become increasingly more difficult with your child.

I do suggest having a last minute emergency escape hatch in the form of rewarding them for good behavior from earlier in the day (when they were fresh and more cooperative). For example, I might say, "Well, since you did such a good job straightening up your room, I'm going to let you off the hook. Will you promise me that you will do this for me first thing in the morning when I ask you to?" They always say yes. You will need this escape hatch when you and your child are just too tired (or sick) to continue. You will be firm and stick to your guns as much as you possibly can, but I want you to also get a sense for when to let yourself (and your child) off the hook.

Clapping	Paint
Computer	Piggy Toes
Cookie	Playing Trains
Cracker Snack	Poker Chips
Cuddling	Ring Around the Rosy
Give Favorite Blanket	Special Toy
Hug	Pouring
Ice Cream	Stickers
Kisses	Storybook
Lollipop	"That's Just Fine"
Making Faces	Tickle
Milk	Trip to the Park
Movement Game	TV
Music Tape	Water/ Sand Play
	"You did a great job!"

A reward can be anything if it meets the following criteria:

- **Your child wants it bad enough to work for it, and**

- **Your child considers it a special treat** (and not just you). For example, toys picked on "on sale" generally do not work because they are not specifically desired by your child. Don't waste money on typical party treats unless your child *really* likes those things.

> **Your Child Must Want a Reward Bad Enough to Work for It.**
>
> **Pick something THEY like instead of something you like or that's on sale.**

Safe Consequences

First, make sure your child is not sick (by taking them to the doctor) if they begin to tantrum more than usual and you are not introducing a schedule change.

Second, use physical movement as a consequence to get them to do what you need them to and to serve as a deterrent. Examples of this include:

- Ball bouncing, balloon hits, jumping,
- Toe touches, sit ups, push-ups, Jumping Jacks
- Writing sorry cards (they can trace over your writing if they are still learning to read and write)

If your child tends to the defiant and won't cooperate at all, Dr. James Dobson has written many books on the proper use of discipline. If at all possible, have them exhaust all of their tantrum energy doing physical exercise instead of venting it toward you. With older kids, the cycle can be repeated until they are worn down (but not to the point of exhaustion). Always build in breaks to give your child a moment to compose himself before repeating the behavior for which he is in trouble. Something like sitting on the stairs and reading his Bible is in order here as opposed to a play break or television viewing.

If your child is becoming calmer but still won't comply, gently place your hands on top of his and physically walk him through the job. (Be nice here. You're not trying to punish you child with this guidance.) Stop when he starts to comply. Praise him immediately for his new compliance. If he stops complying because you're being nice to him; stop and return to guiding him through the task.

> **If Your Home Life is Miserable,**
>
> **It's Probably Because Your Child is In Charge**

Schedule for Very Young Children

As you learn to create and implement lesson trees, you will be able to build more learning interaction to your day. When you child is very young, a 15-minute "lesson" done on the hour will suffice and provide you with much encouragement. Whenever you add a new theme, you will add another new 15-minute "lesson" onto another hour of your child's day. That way, you still have time to attend to household duties and other family needs (not to mention that your child's physical needs are still in the forefront at this stage).

Reward your child right away when he does a good job for you. Your rewards will be heavy at first and then you will gradually ease the rewards out over time. If he starts to backslide, go back to the previous reward expectation.

Instead of punishing a young child, I prefer a form of redirection. For example, if they won't work on a puzzle with you, then you have them bounce a ball 5 times (or something else that is hard, but not impossible, for them to do and for which they could use the practice) and then try again to have them do the puzzle. Repeat as necessary.

Be careful in picking up and comforting a child that is having a tantrum unless you're trying to reward them for having a tantrum! If you need to restrain a young child, seat them face out on your forearm with your other arm across their chest. Have their head slightly to the side of your face leaning on your shoulder so that, if they slam their head back, their head will hit your shoulder instead of your mouth.

Some children will delight in hearing Mom wince (when they slam into your chest, for example) and you must take immediate action in setting a personal boundary if you don't want to be hurt in the future.

Make sure that there is a dramatic difference between your expressions so you child is clear on your mood. For example, exaggerate your smile (happy) or your brows (mad) or your mouth (sad) when providing your child with feedback.

Supplementary Skills

The following list contains other skills you may need to work on with your child in order to get them to the point where they can learn from you.

- Paying attention to you when you speak,
- Looking at what you are trying to show them (if they look away, place your flat hand in front of their eyes, but not touching their eyes, until they return their gaze to you), and
- Not grabbing your teaching items (if they do and won't let go, tickle them under their arm until they release it).
- When you're trying to get them to talk, use something they really like. For example, show them a car and say, "car."

Repeat. When he says "car," give him the car to play with as his reward.

- Stay in charge and in control. First, he does what you want him to do. After he complies with your wishes, then, you may comply with his.

Summer Schedule Example

9:00 a.m.	Wake, dress, eat
9:30 a.m.	Make bed, clean room
10:00 a.m.	Chore
11:00 a.m.	Watch math video , feed cat
11:30 a.m.	Handwriting
12:00 noon	Lunch Break
12:30 p.m.	Go pool
3:00 p.m.	Free time
4:00 p.m.	Break
5:15 p.m.	Chore
6:00 p.m.	Dinner
6:30 p.m.	Load dishwasher
7:00 p.m.	Take out trash
7:30 p.m.	Shower
8:00 p.m.	Floss, brush and use mouth wash
9:00 p.m.	Bedtime

VI. Captivation of Brilliance

It is crucial that you begin to get a feel for your child's genuine likes and dislikes. Expect surprises along the way. You may put together a beautiful "cowboy/farm" lesson only to discover that your child has moved on to trucks. Astonishingly, you may discover that you've hit it just right and your child's vocabulary and knowledge expand very quickly and the information sticks.

Cross-Referencing Materials

After you've collected a few teacher's guides, textbooks, posters, and toys for different subject areas, you may begin to feel overwhelmed with all the materials.

Gather some medium-sized boxes and sort your toys, games and books in the boxes based on major themes such as Africa, farm, Earth science, etc. The only other organizing you will need to come up with is a cross-reference list for your teaching books as, many times, there are several themes contained in one book (and you don't want to have to look through all of your books each time you put a theme together).

> Earth Day
> - SB1 – 31 – What a Wonderful World bulletin board using Louis Armstrong Song
> - SC – 113 – Creation Station – recycling
> - LCB – 251 – vocabulary and activities
> - BV – community – 24 – recycle center
> - OCW

Give each of your books an abbreviation and list the page number where the theme information is found. If you prefer to be very organized, you can create a quick reference list of everything that's in your theme box so that you can refer to it easily.

Creating Your Own Materials

For each new theme that you create, you will want to put together a one-sheet picture (find pictures on the internet) reference sheet containing the 3-5 most important things that you want your child to learn. Review the sheet whenever you begin a lesson from that theme.

Don't be overly concerned with creating professional looking materials for your child. The goal is to make them fun and engaging for your child. Color usually helps but the most important thing to your child, as shown in the writing example that follows, is that the subject matter be interesting to them. Sometimes, too, handwritten materials can be more "memorable" to a child than something printed out from the computer. Also, no one will see your materials except for your child (unless you actually write a book!).

> **Working Title:** _(handwritten)_
>
> | Characters | Setting |
> |---|---|
> | _(handwritten)_ | Scene 1: _(handwritten)_ |
> | | Scene 2: _(handwritten)_ |
> | | Scene 3: _(handwritten)_ |
>
> **Plot**
>
> | Beginning | Middle | End |
> |---|---|---|
> | _(handwritten)_ | _(handwritten)_ | _(handwritten)_ |

For a writing exercise like this, don't focus on correcting minor errors if the child needs encouragement just to continue. If they've had many writing setbacks to reach this point and this is the first time your child has felt successful, allow him the opportunity to begin to thin of writing as fun. Build their self-confidence and enjoyment of the activity before offering any type of correction. Note that the main organizational ideas stand out due to the handwritten and easy-to-read headings.

Over time, you will become more and more comfortable creating your own worksheets. Be sure and either cover a worksheet you make in a clear plastic report cover (the kind that have a colored removable spine) so that you can use dry erase markers with it, or make several copies before giving it to your child to use.

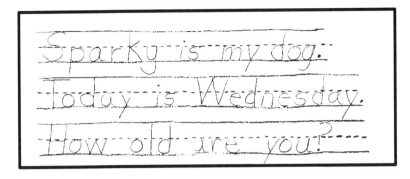

To make worksheets, like the one shown above, more memorable, use colored pencils to create the form and place it in a plastic report cover that your child can use fine point dry erase markers to complete every day.

Using colorful markers to create a form ups its interest factor immediately. Please note that the previous form contained a concept that was difficult for the child, at the time. In this case, you would just work on the tenses for one root word during each lesson and build slowly over time. The child was asked to jump and stop (for jumped), start jumping and keep jumping while saying "jumping," and then a timer was used to illustrate the concept of "will jump" in the future. Always act out any verbs with your child to help solidify their understanding of the word.

> ### Nouns, Pronouns and Adjectives Song
>
> A noun is a naming word
> for a person, place or thing
> - Jack and Ronnie
> - church and park
> - cookie and toy
>
> These all are naming words.
> A noun is a naming word.
>
> A pronoun is a very short word
> that takes the place of a noun
> - you and yours
> - me, mine and I
> - it and them
>
> These are all very short words
> that take the place of a noun.
>
> An adjective is a describing word
> that tells you more about a noun.
> - blue and red
> - sad and bad
> - big and six
>
> These are words that tell you more
> about a person, place or thing.

Take any children's song, that is familiar to you and your child, and adapt it to use as an aid in teaching your child a concept. No, they don't get the songs confused as the words and ideas are so very different. Knowing the tune frees up your child to focus on the learning idea. This song was sung to the tune of "Old McDonald." Don't worry if it's not perfect. Children tend to be forgiving unless taught to be otherwise.

Customizing Viewing Reels

Many children enjoy using a child's projector and viewing reels as a supplementary tool in learning specific theme information. These can be used for genuine learning if you list the slide number and title (shown on the outside in the middle of the reel) and add research notes beforehand. For example, if you're looking at a space theme reel, research rocketry so that you can discuss the various parts of the rocket that are shown on the slide.

Cross-Subject Inclusive Green Lesson Tree

The following chapter offers many games and activities, as well as a party, related to specific (fun) cross-combined themes. The Green Lesson Tree that follows gives you the subject breakdown for each theme. Ideas for activities in each subject area follow as well. See the chapter entitled, "Techniques for Three to Seven Year Olds," for completed lesson tree examples.

<u>Reading & Writing</u>

- Read a storybook that includes the theme,
- Read a nonfiction book about the theme,
- Research and write a report on the theme,
- Pretend to be a character in the story and write out your own version of the tale, and
- Come up with a song or rhyme to remember important information.

<u>Social Studies</u>

- Read about the time period/culture in which the story occurs.
- Watch a video about the country
- Try out some of the foods from the country or period
- Research games and activities the characters might have played in the story.

Science

- Pick out a scientific feature of the story to cover. For example, weather might be an appropriate subject for the "Greek Mythology & The Hercules Fraction Flip" cross-theme in that Zeus likes to throw around thunderbolts.

- If your child likes the ocean and ocean animals, Poseidon and the sea might be a more appropriate focus for scientific study.

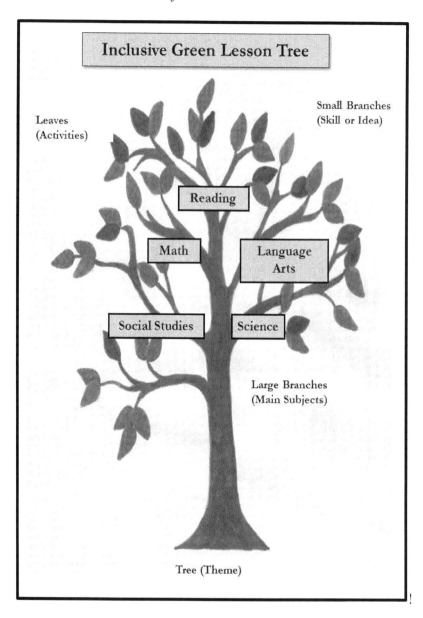

Achieving Brilliance at Home

VII. Mathematics of Brilliance

WARNING

Most of the following math lessons conclude with an air gun arcade. It is recommended that everyone present at the arcade wear eye goggles. Do not use valued toys for the targets as they may become broken during play. Place the arcade table about two feet away from a wall or other obstruction and place exercise mats on the floor between the wall and the table to assist in the preservation of toys that fall on the floor.

Never allow more than one child to use the air gun at a time. Use only one air gun and three air darts at a time. Collect all toys that have fallen and air darts *before* giving the next child a loaded air gun at the arcade. **Never shoot an air gun at a rubberized object, like a balloon, and it may bounce back and cause injury. When in doubt, have everyone wear eyes goggles for safety.**

The air gun target practice is presented in the spirit of an old-fashioned arcade and in no way endorses the harm of any animal. An air gun game that involves the shooting of stuffed animals represents "tranquilizing darts in order that the animals that have invaded a populated city may be relocated to the wild."

* * *

The following games were created to assist in preparing children for their 5th Grade math testing, which determined whether they went on to middle school, and can be built around a movie of your choice. The movie is shown at the end of all activities (time permitting) to enhance the fun of the games. Feel free to adapt themes. Always adapt games and party activities to the likes of your child.

The games may be adapted for a younger child by simply making the activities easier. Use the lesson examples shown in the front of your purchased math textbook to create the games and activities. Use your curriculum or textbook as a guide in adapting the activities for your particular child or children.

Alice in Wonderland & Problem Solving

Typically, Alice in Wonderland is used for a Valentine's Day party and is preferred by girls. However, your boys can dress up as knights or playing cards and, of course, you will have one boy dress up as the Mad Hatter. The air gun activity at the after-party is also for the boys (but the girls had fun with it as well).

In the back of your mind, think of the Mad Hatter as a stylized clown (orange wig, face make-up, clog shoes). If you decide to make this a public event, garner attendees by having breakfast in a public restaurant (in costume) *before* your event begins. Put a name tag on your Mad Hatter to avoid strange looks and to indicate your event will be held at ____ and will begin at ____. "See you there." Your Mad Hatter could engage younger children if you go light on the clown and heavy on the charm.

Achieving Brilliance at Home

The following chart displays the materials you will need in order to prepare your sessions. Items designated by an asterisk (*) must be prepared beforehand.

Note that themed border paper is suggested for each session, but you only need five (5) sheets of paper. You will cover these theme-bordered sheets in a plastic report cover (the type with colored removable spines) to use for problem solving using dry erase markers. Laminate these sheets if you're planning on using them more than once.

Pre-Event	Mad Hatter Costume	Valentine's Day Tea Party	Games & Activities	After-Party
Determine Location	Button down shirt	Cups	Chess Set	Air gun with light pointer
Flyers & Posters	Black fitted jacket	Napkins	Cheshire Cat Paper Plates*	Red tablecloth
Sign-In Sheet	Men's Dress Socks	Plates	Knights & Castle Toob,	Flag streamers*
Money Handler	Black clog-type shoes	Candy	Sabuda Castle Book	Mini-canopy*
Helper Teachers	Thick fabric for bow tie.	White tablecloth	Playing Cards	Give away prizes
Take Home Cards*	Orange clown wig	Math Textbook	Hearts Bordered Paper	Digital Camera
Magician's Hat & cloth for band hat	Clown face paints	Teapot, Creamer & Sugar Bowl	3 baskets for stacking	Red, pink and white paper
Size-card for hat*	Cupcakes		3-5 stuffed animals	Winding ribbon
	Drinks			

> Items designated with an asterisk (*) need to be made beforehand.

Other Costume Ideas

Alice	Hare	Sleepy Dormouse	Queen/King of Hearts	Cheshire Cat	Gryphon/Jabberwocky
Blue dress	Jacket	Pajamas	Crown	Old-fashioned drawn on whiskers	Head, talons, and wings of an eagle and the body of a lion
White apron	Pocket watch		Red silky cloth used as a cape or skirt	Black or brown clothing	or a Dragon (a mix of several different animals in the original story)

Pre-Event

Determine Location: If you are not holding the event at home, you will want to scout out locations such as community centers, churches, etc. If you are a home school family, this is a great opportunity to get to know other homeschoolers and people in your community.

Pre-Event

Flyers & Posters: Create flyers and colorful and engaging posters and post them one-two weeks in advance to get people excited about your event. If you need an all-day or all-week event, you could read through the book and then watch and discuss the various movie adaptations. (See example at the top of this chapter heading.)

Sign-In Sheet: Keep track of your attendees so that you can contact them directly for future events or track the sessions they participated in to determine whether the sessions are effectively introducing, teaching, reteaching or reviewing the skills you intended.

Money Handler: If you charge for your event, you will need to have someone available to handle money changing and/or ticket redemption.

Helper Teachers: If possible, you will set up all games and activities at tables, cover them with a tablecloth, and have a helper teacher sit at the table until the students are ready for that activity. You will set up the tables and teach your table helper how to perform the activity beforehand. If your activities are simple and engaging enough, this can be done just before the session begins. You will also need to point out to your helper where the hidden answers are on the materials.

Instruct them not to point out the hidden answers to the children at first. The children usually catch on quickly and this takes a lot of the tension out of the activities for everyone. Just make sure that you have the children try to solve the problem before they are allowed to look at the answer. The mood should be fast and fun and give students the idea that *this* math is actually fun. You may follow up with worksheets or book homework if you've used your

Pre-Event
textbook examples to create the materials (which is what I suggest). **Cheshire Cat Take Home Cards:** I always like to have students review one set of times tables at each session. For this particular session, I drew a free-hand Cheshire Cat face onto paper plates and had students color and complete it with their name. On the backside of the paper plates, the students wrote out the times table set they had just been pop-quizzed on as a group. If someone didn't know the answer, I'd say, "Let's help him out," (said in a fun and jovial way) and everyone would yell the correct answer jumping and laughing (as they all looked at the poster showing the correct answers that had been overlooked before). Then, they would complete the back of their Cheshire Cat in crayon (so the colors wouldn't bleed through).

Mad Hatter Costume
Black Magician's hat: Can be found at a party store or online
Cloth to band hat: Any color fabric that is cut into a strip long enough to tie in the back and hang down.
Small size-card for hat: I used a piece of manila file folder. See photo for example of what to write or look at original book.
Button-down shirt: neutral color
Black fitted jacket: thrift shops usually have these available
Men's dress socks: these should be knee socks so that you can put them on and then roll up the legs of black sweat pants so that they end just below the knee.
Black shoes: Dutch-looking shoes work well.

Mad Hatter Costume

Thick fabric to make large bow tie: Stiffer fabric works best. Measure a rectangle of fabric around your Hatter's neck so that the ends fall about chest level. Accordion pleat the rectangle and tie it into a loose double knot around their neck. Slightly open the accordion pleats if needed.

Orange clown wig: if you want to tone down the shiny orange color, spray paint the ends of the wig with temporary orange hair color typically found at a party store. Let dry before using wig.

Clown face paints: I painted my Hatter's face white (except for his eyes) and used cosmetics to complete the other features.

Valentine's Day Tea Party

Cupcakes: You can either make these or buy them already made from the store. Just try to keep to your hearts theme. Alternatively, a cake works just as well except for the additional mess and effort. Also, have some fruit available for those students for whom sweets are inappropriate.

Drinks: Make sure you offer an alternative to cola and punch such as bottle water.

Cups, napkins and plates: Valentine's Day themed paper products are nice or you can just use red merchandise. The teapot, creamer and sugar bowl will be used for one of the math activities which you will prepare beforehand.

Candy: The Mad Hatter will give out heart-shaped candy for correct answers on one of the math games.

> **White tablecloth:** I recommend white to contrast with the red or heart-themed paper products.

Games & Activities

Math textbook: You will create your games using the examples given in your textbook to solve specific math problems. You may then follow-up during the week with worksheets or homework problems taken from the appropriate section in the book. Make sure that your homework correlates to the correct lesson if your session covers all of the lessons in a unit. For the purpose of this book, you *will not* stand in the front of the room and use a lecture format while writing on the board (ever!).

Each table helper teacher will instruct the students (in waves) as to the way each game or activity is played. She will use her dry erase sheets (instructions on how to make these follow) to write out the activity using different colored markers. She will have each student do a very easy problem on their own.

My purpose for these activities is (1) to create an automatic memory pathway as to the steps taken to solve a problem, and (2) to engage the student in an activity that reframes math as a fun activity in their mind. This is not the time for a hard stance on getting the students to perform the hardest problems available in order to earn the prize party at the end. You will reinforce these sessions with worksheets and homework during the week and, if necessary, you can repeat the entire session several times.

Please do exactly the same activities the second go around so that your students can gain confidence through the activities that they now find easy (even if from memory if they can work out the steps) and feel encouraged to see if there are still problems they find difficult.

The party is used as an incentive to get them to perform all activities and no student is allowed to just sit and watch and then attend the party.

Games & Activities

Clear report covers and stationery: Buy several packs of inexpensive, glossy, and clear report covers (the kind that have detachable colored plastic spines). I don't recommend laminating stationery for this use unless you can find stationery that will work with every theme you plan to use. (Please note that the back side will always be plain white or you may want to double-side themes and then laminate.) Remove the spine and take a piece of Valentine's Day, border-design only, stationery and place it the cover. Staple it two times only on the outside, open, edge. You will use these in lieu of dry erase boards. Do not use the spine.

Dry erase markers: You will need several packs of these, as well as paper towels or dry erasers, for the students to use to figure out problems. Each student will have a (1) dry erase marker, (2) an eraser/paper towel, and (3) a dry erase plastic cover containing an attractive sheet of theme stationery. These can either stay at each table for the students to use as they rotate in or they can be assigned and carried by each student.

Cheshire Cat Plates: Locate an illustration of the Cheshire Cat, make several copies, and paste it to the outside (round part – like a face) of a paper plate or let students free-hand draw their own Cheshire Cat and then color it with their own hair color, eye color, etc. These can be used to write out their set of multiplication facts for the session and/or for teacher helpers to keep track of correct answers so they can choose their chess piece later (such as king or queen) or win a prize at the end.

Teapot: Using your math textbook, locate <u>word problem</u> examples for each lesson. Decide on about 4-5 examples you will use. Print them out onto light brown paper in such a way that the sheet of paper can be folded into booklet form and then cut into raindrop shapes. (You are *not* trying to retain the booklet usage here.) On a white sheet of paper, print out your problem on a smaller raindrop and affix to drop of tea. Write answer on the back of the tea drop. If there are a number of steps involved,

Games & Activities

make sure helper teacher has a copy of the actual examples handy. *Make sure the answer key is very handy. Ideally, the answer is hidden somewhere on the back of the raindrop.* Have child work out their problem on their dry erase sheet and then check it against your answer key. Remember, this exercise is to help them remember the ***steps*** to solving their problem so the same example can be used over and over again, until they've gained confidence, and then they can apply their new skill to a new problem.

Sugar Bowl: Remember, "**Eat Me**," made Alice **larger** so you will print out math problems that involve larger answers (such as in **addition** and **multiplication**). *These do not have to be word problems.* Print the problems out on construction paper or card stock so that they can be folded over like a booklet. Cut the booklets into circles to resemble little cakes retaining a small spine. Yes, these *are* cover page and back page fold-over booklets. Decorate the top of the "cakes" with crayons or glitter which will be allowed to dry overnight. **Make sure you have the words, "Eat Me," written on the decorated outside top of the "little cake."** I do not suggest using markers because they will bleed through the construction paper or card stock. Hide the answer on the back of the card (or even somewhere on top in the decoration), but make sure your student shows the steps on their dry erase sheet in order to get credit. The question is revealed inside when you open the cover

Creamer Pitcher: Remember, "**Drink Me**," made Alice **smaller** so you will print out math problems that involve smaller answers (such as in **subtraction** and **division**). Outline the shape of a small bottle laying on its side. This will be your shape pattern for the little booklets so make sure the problems print out small enough to fit on the inside of your "bottle." You will also want to make sure that your bottle shapes are small enough to fit into your creamer pitcher. Don't forget to write, **"Drink Me,"** on the top of the cards.

Achieving Brilliance at Home

Games & Activities

Chess Set: Cut out squares the shape and size of the last two rows of each side of the chess board. On one side of the little card, you will free-hand draw a chess piece (this side will be face-down as it <u>serves as the student's answer key</u>) and add a number to differentiate each pawn.

On the other side of the card will be the number of the corresponding chess piece. You can either print out the problem, hole punch it, and attach it to the chess piece using a rubber band (thread the rubber band through the card hole and back through itself and then place the free circle end over the chess piece) or you can affix the problem to the bottom of the chess piece.

Child solves problem using dry erase sheets and then checks his answer by guessing which answer matches his problem. He flips card to see if he has the correct "pawn" (for example).

Create an incentive whereby the student gets to be the king, queen, etc., based on the number of correct answers they get. Helper teachers could track this on the back of their Cheshire Cat paper plates.

Knights and Dragon Toob® by Safari Ltd®

Toy Knights, Chess Board and Playing Cards: Have students pick out a knight that will advance one space for each correct answer. Student draws a playing card from the deck, writes it out on their dry erase sheet, helper teacher confirms answer, and student's knight advances one place.

Jeanne Mifflin

Castle: Medieval Days and Knights (A Sabuda & Reinhart Pop-up Book)

Castle and pop-up book: Hide problem cards in the folds of an elaborate pop-up book (*Castle*, Sabuda & Reinhart). After child has worked out the answer on dry erase sheet, there is a clue on the back of the card that leads them to a steeple on the castle where they can check their answer (which is being held by a magician, dragon, knight with a sword, etc.). Child should react appropriately to the character when they check their answer. "He just burned me," "He just stabbed me with his sword," and "He just turned me into a dog," at which point student begins to walk on all fours until his correct answer is confirmed.

Mad Hatter's Playing Cards: Mad Hatter doles out one card to one child at a time (and has his corresponding answer card hidden in his pocket). Helper teacher helps student (if necessary) work out answer on dry erase sheets and Hatter reveals pocket card at end or student may pull card from Hatter's pocket to check their answer. If they get the answer right, the Hatter gives them a piece of candy.

After-Party

Three (3) Baskets For Stacking: I used apple crates for this purpose. You will stack these, pyramid-style, on top of a table with two baskets next to each other creating the bottom and one basket in the middle on top. See "African Safari" chapter for photo. Cover with a silky red cloth. This will create two levels on which to stand Valentine's Day stuffed animals.

Three (3) to five (5) Stuffed Animals: The cuter and more Valentine's Day-themed these stuffed animals are, the more your boys will get a kick out of shooting them with air guns. Girls don't seem to be overly sensitive and, if you're using an air gun with a sight (which is what I suggest), they also enjoy the shooting arcade. Each student will have three tries to shoot an animal off its level. (**Notes:** When in doubt, use eye goggles. *Do not* use treasured stuffed animals as targets as they will probably become damaged with heavy use.)

Air Gun with Light Pointer: I suggest placing your arcade table about two feet out (running lengthwise) from a wall and placing barrier chairs at each end so no child can enter the arcade backdrop. It makes it easier for you to retrieve air darts and stuffed animals if there is space behind the table. Only one student goes at a time to help you maintain control of the arcade.

Red Silky Tablecloth: This is draped over apple baskets for a dramatic display. Please note that, if the bottom of your baskets are uneven (which are used as platforms for your targets), you may need to place cardboard circles underneath your cloth to help stabilize the stuffed animals. You may tuck extra fabric under the baskets or leave puddled at the bottom.

Flag Streamers: Cut out red triangle flag shapes from construction paper and staple them along a length of curling or other ribbon that is then taped to the wall behind the arcade table and secured to the tabletop for decoration.

After-Party

Mini-Canopy: Cut a red piece of construction paper in half lengthwise. Cut a white piece of construction paper in half lengthwise. Cut one end of the halves into a semi-circle shape. Glue halves together, alternating colors, to create a red and white scalloped edge mini-canopy. You will affix this to the arcade wall to cover or embellish the two canopy ribbon ends.

Give Away Prizes: Have a good supply of pencils and other give-aways available as prizes. For the arcades, depending on the skill level of your shooters, you may want to only offer prizes if they get all three animals (1 animal on each of their three tries).

Digital Camera: After the shooting arcade is over, you may want to offer photographs to children as an incentive to return to the next session. Your Valentine's Day arcade makes a great backdrop for photos. This works particularly well if your attendees decided to come in costume (for which they would need about two weeks notice). Children will pick up their photos at their next math session.

Achieving Brilliance at Home

African Safari Rescue & Decimal Quest

Find a great movie you can use for inspiration for this unit. The one I used pulled police and other rescue vehicles into the story along with African savannah and Congo River animals. Be sure and have your safari-costumed students make a tour of your facility or visit a nearby restaurant to promote your event in the hours just before it is held. If you need to fill a couple of hours when the after-party is over, watching the movie can be a great extension of the session.

The following chart displays the materials you will need in order to prepare for your sessions.

Pre-Event	Costumes	Food & Beverage	After-Party
Determine Location	Australian hat, sunglasses, and tan shirt	Cupcakes or Theme Cake	3 baskets for stacking
Flyers & Posters	Pith helmet or hat, long tan button and pockets shirt, brown belt with large buckle fastened over shirt, toy shotgun	Drinks	7-9 medium-sized plastic African animals
Sign-In Sheet		Cups	
		Napkins	
Money Handler	(Safariology - Safari Ltd., has great costume props.)	Plates	Air gun with light pointer
Helper Teachers	Police costume – all one color pants and shirt tucked and belted with fake gun and badge, police helmet, police station and mini-cars		Give away prizes
Take Home Cards			Digital Camera
	Fireman costume – hat, jacket, face mask, etc.		

If you have trouble seeing the take-home card that follows, scan it or enlarge it for viewing. You may feel free to use the card for your needs.

Alternatively, if you'd would like to make your own, capture pictures from the internet in order to create an engaging (and, prefereably, colored) card through which your child and fondly remember their session (and, hopefully, the skills they learned).

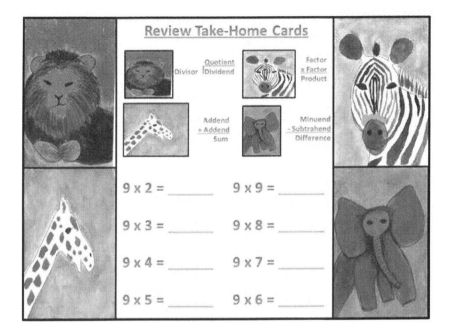

Try to come up with a cute take home card for each session. Teacher helper notes would be shown on the back of each student's card. If you copy and enlarge the take-home card above, please point out that the answers reverse each other. For example, 9 x 2 = 18, 9 x 9 = 81.

The following table displays the materials you will need to create your games and activities. **Please note that the game INSTRUCTIONS follow the materials list in a separate table.**

Games & Activities Supplies Needed
Math Textbook: Use lesson examples to create games as appropriate. These games are based on decimal practice. Feel free to adapt the games to suit your child's grade and ability and your specific purpose.

Games & Activities Supplies Needed

Congo Rescue: Large stuffed animal snake, large blue sheet, jungle theme blow-up life preserver and alligator, rope to tie around life preserver to rescue students from river, about 20 stones of three difference types, prepared number line and game cards (see example in game description that follows)

Charging Elephants: 6-8 plastic elephant figures, construction paper, markers

Motorcycle Monkeys: Large motorcycle rider on functional wheels, plastic monkeys that hook, dry erase sheets and markers (see Alice in Wonderland for instructions on how to make dry erase sheets).

March and Eat Ants: Construction paper in green, brown, tan, a couple of toy ants

Multiplying Dragonflies: Construction paper in yellow, orange, green and blue, black and red fine point markers, dark brown crayon

Police & Fireman Badge Flips: 6-8 toy fire and police badges or these can be made from cardstock, black markets, gold or yellow marker

Games & Activities Supplies Needed

Dividing Decimals Monkey: 4 pieces of orange construction paper or one large sheet, green construction paper, brown construction paper, black marker, white crayon, 3 poker chips, make the following letters using a Bodoni 350 font out of white card stock – make three 1's, make two 2's, make two 3's, make one 0.

Fireman Rescue Puzzle: Firehouse puzzle; fireman props such as a face mask, Chief's hat, toy ax, etc., along with small replica fireman's tools.

Fireman Prop: Toy accessory kit where fire tools snap into frame.

Games & Activities Instructions

Math Textbook: Use problem examples on the first pages of each lesson to create games and activities as appropriate. These games are based on decimal practice. Exact models have been provided to give you an idea of how to set up your games. Feel free to adapt them to your needs. In the week following the session, use the textbook to come up with homework and worksheets to reinforce the skills learned at the session.

If you make a mistake, *let the students catch it*. Correcting YOU is one of the most fun ways for THEM to learn. Note the displaced 8.13 and 8.12. Don't get flustered, laugh about it!

> **Congo Rescue:** Lay out the blue bed sheet to represent the Congo River. Use blow-up alligator and stuffed snake as props only in the pretend water. Take about 20 stones of three difference types of rock and prepare number stones and game cards as follows. (Game shown in previous photos.) Create two sets of number cards for your number stones game. Cut both sets apart while keeping the numbers in sequence.
>
> The first set is affixed to your stone groupings and the second set is cut apart and used as draw cards from a small fish bowl. Compare all stone numbers with your child *before* you start the game. After previewing the stones, turn them all face down

EXCEPT for the first stone in the row. Don't forget to place the stones in the Congo river in rows.

One student at a time enters the river and, after they've found the correct rock that correlates to their card, they are thrown the life preserver which is attached to a rope to pull them out. Alternatively, they can throw the life preserve to catch the head of a blow-up monkey to free them from the river.

Charging Elephants: Create place mat and small cards as shown previously. Tape to plastic elephant figures. Mix all of the elephants up and have students put them in the proper positioning while teaching YOU the differences between the positions.

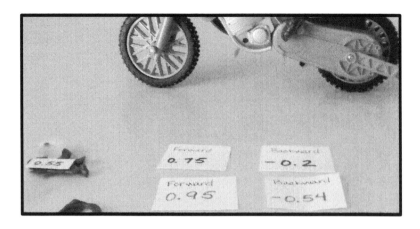

Motorcycle Monkeys: (See previous photo.) Child uses dry erase sheet to work out decimal subtraction problem matching card sets. (Write the sets out in different colors to make them easier to match up at the session.) Once the correct answer corresponding monkey has been found, it is hooked to the motorcycle rider. After all problems have been solved, the motorcycle rider is then pushed to another child waiting at the end of the table and the game aims to see how many of the monkeys get knocked off during the run. (See Alice in Wonderland for instructions on how to make dry erase sheets.)

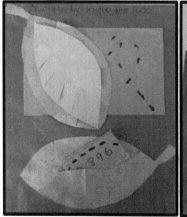
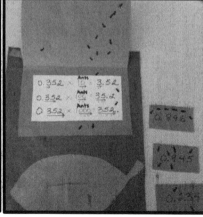

Achieving Brilliance at Home

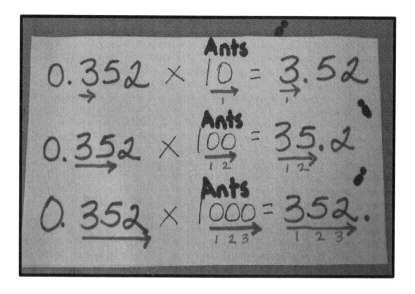

March and Eat Ants: Create game kit, as shown above, with problem cards stored in the lower leaf. Top leaf is attached to top of fold-over card that reveals the rules for multiplying decimals by 10, 100 and 100- along with an example of each. Carefully go over explanatory card with students. Afterward, give a student a game card (shown in previous photos) and have them determine the correct position for the decimal. Have a jumbo plastic ant sitting on top leaf of game when it is set out as a prop if desired. Another alternative would be to write a mystery rhyme as to what the game is about as a decoration for the top leaf.

If you have time and would like to perfect your sets with elaborate graphics, etc., feel free to do so if you can justify the time. Laminating, computer-printed instructions, etc., would be very appropriate if you plan to teach several children over the course of several years.

From my experience, imperfections almost seem to make the games more memorable so be sure and allow a few imperfections on which the child can memory log.

 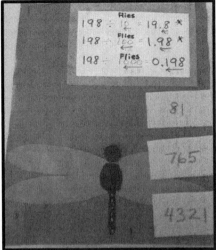

Multiplying Dragonflies: Create dragonfly motif as shown above by cutting and gluing construction paper. Make the top rectangle a fold-over card as shown. Leave a slit at the top of your dragonfly to hold playing cards that you prepare as shown. Explain to students the idea that, if you want to divide and number by 10, you simply move the decimal point one place left. Do the same for dividing by 100 and 1000. Have student repeat back to you the concept and then tell you where the decimal points should be for each playing card.

Achieving Brilliance at Home

Dividing Decimals: Be a sure to write the correct answer on the back of your playing cards or worksheet.J

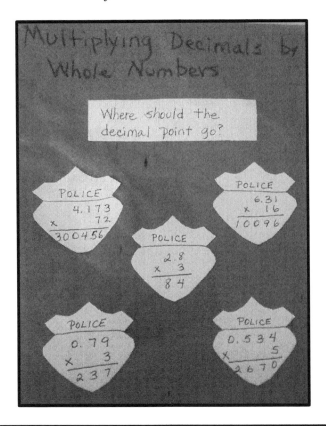

Police Badge Multiplication: Affix problems to small white cards and affix to 4-6 toy police badges or make from cardstock as shown above. Answers will be noted on the back of the badges or written on the back of the problem sheets. Remember, this exercise is merely to have students practice placing their decimals so they can move through that quickly when solving real problems.

Liven up this game by assigning each student a mini-car. If they get a wrong answer, their car goes into the police impound until they have another turn and get the correct answer. Teacher Helper can wear a police helmet and gear to make it more fun. If they get the correct answer, they can race their cars off the end of a table onto an exercise mat or into the hands of another

Achieving Brilliance at Home

> child placed at the end of the table. Be sure there is plenty of clearance at the end of table and/or that cars land on something soft. Position cars and children in such a way that cars are not directed toward the face of another child, windows, etc. If there is enough space, have your students race their cars across the room. Make sure you set up a starting line and a finish line.

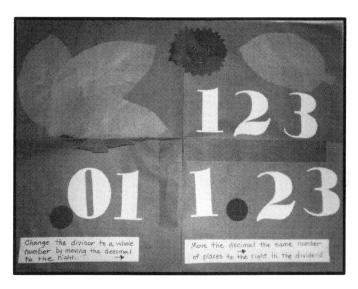

Dividing Decimals Fireman: Explain to your child that, when you are dividing decimals, you must turn the divisor into a whole number first. Advise them to do the same for the dividend which reflects in the quotient. Have the fireman move the poker chip to help them remember to move the decimal point.. Have your child repeat the instructions back to you before performing the task. Make sure your child uses the fireman to move the poker chip in order to help them remember.

Fireman Rescue Puzzle: Outline around puzzle pieces onto white paper to make the problem cards for any puzzle relating to the theme. On the back, of the actual puzzle pieces themselves, write the correct answers. The puzzle pieces stay face down on the table until it's time to do the answer check. Child works the problems out on a dry erase sheet.

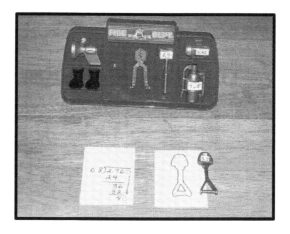

Fireman Rescue Props: Outline around prop pieces onto white paper to make the problem cards. On the reverse of the prop card, write out a problem as shown in photo. Affix a tiny card showing the correct answer to the prop and place it back in frame. After student works out answer on a dry erase sheet, he selects the prop he thinks has the correct answer. Student then flips his problem card over to reveal the correct answer shape and verifies that prop and answer outline match.

After-Party

After students have *completed* ALL activities, they enjoy treats to begin the after party.

A table is then set up two feet from a wall lengthwise (with a chair blocking entrance at each end) to stack three apple baskets (or crates) into a pyramid and then cover with savannah grass looking fabric as shown in picture.

Another table is set up two feet lengthwise from the first that students stand behind to aim and shoot "tranquilizer darts" into the animals so that the animals can be relocated to the vet or released back into the wild. An air gun with a sight works best for this target practice. If a child knocks off an animal during all three of their tries, he or she (girls like this game too) gets a prize (like a pencil or pencil sharpener) or a ticket for a drawing to be held later.

Alternatively, you can take your child outside and have them shoot stuffed animals out of trees using "tranquilizer darts" (air darts) so that the animals can be relocated to the wild. When in doubt, have your child wear eye goggles.

Be sure and take photos to incentivize children to return for the next session. See if you can get their parents to go ahead and sign them up so you can be "sure" and have their photo ready.

Achieving Brilliance at Home

Valley of the Kings & The Geometry Curse

Setting & Story Line: Child has an overnight sleepover party at an orbiting planet space museum. The party is part of an experiment that tests the new artificial intelligence problem-solving ability of the computer that maintains the museum. The museum is known for its virtual reality walls and animated holographic images.

Alternatively, find a movie that matches this particular theme such as a movie about the Egyptian Pharaohs, Ancient Egypt, etc., or come up with your own simple story line.

Pre-Event	Costumes	Snacks	Games & Activities	After-Party
Determine Location Flyers &	**Pharoah** – Brilliantly colored construction	Cupcakes, Popcorn, etc.	Math Textbook	3 baskets to stack

Posters Sign-In Sheet	paper, winding ribbon, glitter	Drinks	Cube light box and pegs, plain thermal paper,	See photo of poster at chapter heading.
Money Handler	**Queen** – gold pipe cleaners, white sheet, sandals, gold jewelry, kohl eye shadow	Cups Napkins Plates	Child's screen projector and image cards,	
Helper Teachers				
		Candy	Sheet to cover 3 sides of large table	Digital Camera
Take Home Cards	**Mummy** – strips of white gauze bandage			
			Ancient Egypt Toob (Safari Ltd)	
	Any period or animal costume that can be found in a museum.		Electronic dinosaur and remote control car	
			Yard sale body board or cardboard cut-out,	
			Gold glitter, construction and white paper, glitter markers	
			Dry erase markers	
			Theme border paper & clear covers	

Achieving Brilliance at Home

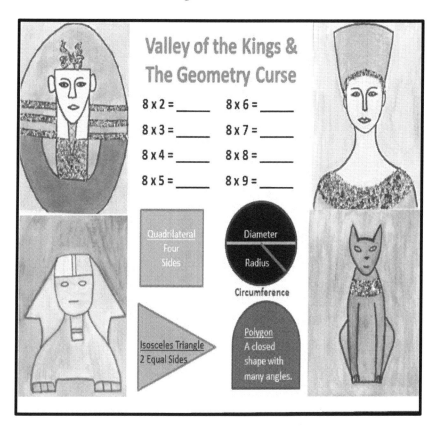

Take-Home Card: Always try to put together some kind of take-home/bulletin board card for your child to help them remember the basic concepts they learned and how much fun they had learning math with you. These should be half-page and printed on card stock. Imperfect images give your students the okay to try new things.

Games & Activities

Math Textbook: Use the examples at the front of the lesson that you want to teach as problems. Create worksheets or use homework problems from the textbook during the following week to reinforce what was learned at the session. Please bear in mind that the aim is to develop memory trails as regards the steps required in order to solve a problem (partial answers may be provided at times). Add varied problems on your worksheets and/or homework to make sure that your child can generalize the problem-solving.

Egyptian Pharoah's Tablet: Take a used body board and paint it with glue. Sprinkle glitter all over the front of it, tap off excess and allow to dry overnight. Cut out large fold-over shapes to make a series of mini-booklets (as shown in previous photos). Print out what you consider to be the most important things for your child to remember on white paper and then cut into shapes matching your construction paper fold-over cutouts. Use glitter pens to decorate, if desired, and let dry overnight. The next day, cut paper into shapes to match fold-over booklets and staple. Glue entire back of booklet to body board and allow to dry overnight.

After children have completed their multiplication practice take home cards, have them take turns reading the pages from the Pharaoh's tablet.

Shape Review: Find photos on the internet depicting the following shapes. You can just enter the shape name (such as "right triangle") and photos will come up. Print out and paste these photos to index cards and state the name of the shape, type of triangle, etc., at the bottom of the card.

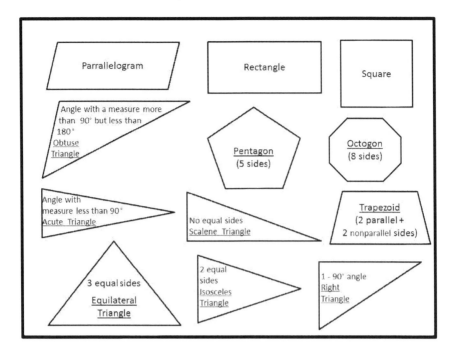

Museum Shape Find: Push a large table against a wall and drape/enclose it with a large dark-colored sheet. Cut out shape cards (shown previously) and place in a container. Have your child draw a card. Child projects viewing reel images onto the wall (while they are under the table, inside the "museum") and look for the shape on their card. After they have found their shape, they show it to you. The shapes can be sought in any viewing reels you have available. Do not hold your child to stringent standards on this activity. You mainly want to get them to start noticing the shapes in everyday life.

Cube Light Angles, Perimeter and Area: Have your child create a closed design on a light cube using thermal paper (preferably) or plain paper cut to size.

Afterward, have your child measure the degree of the angles and count the pegs to determine the area and perimeter.

Monitor your child at all times when the light cube is plugged into an electrical socket.

Ancient Egypt Toob® by Safari Ltd®

Ancient Egypt Toob® by Safari Ltd®

Geometry Curse Board Game: Create a board game for your students to practice their area and perimeter formulas as follows. Use the Ancient Egypt Toob, Safari Ltd., as game pieces for your board game.

1. Cut out a large piece of cardboard in the size and shape of a game board.

2. Cover cardboard with a sheet of gift wrap. Just wrap it like a present using tape as the glue can cause uneven surfaces and puckering of the paper.

3. Create a table on your word processor and make the squares the size of typical game board squares.

4. Cut a blue piece and a yellow piece of construction paper down to the size of 8-1/2 x 11 paper so it will fit into your printer's paper feeder. Print the table with squares out onto one piece of yellow construction paper and one piece of blue construction paper. Cut out all the squares.

5. On a completely empty game board, using tape to assemble colored squares, create a path design working ***opposite*** of the way you want the design to flow on your game board. I just used tape to piece the squares into a path. When finished taping the squares together, turn the "path" over and trim as needed. You can also cut the outside edges for a cleaner finish if you like. Do not glue your path down until you have completed the total layout for your game.

6. Create illustrations of your own or find decorative pictures on the internet. Trim them and continue to plan the lay out of your board game.

7. Make problem playing cards for your game (sphinx on the left as shown in photo). Place them face down on your board game. Make a fold-over answer key for your board game. You may want to affix it to your game so it doesn't get lost (as shown at the bottom and center of the photos.) Let children practice with the cards and self-check their answers before playing an actual game with each other.

Achieving Brilliance at Home

The problem and answer format I used was as follows:

1. How do you find the <u>perimeter</u> of a rectangle?
   a. Add all four sides
   b. Multiply length x width

8. Be sure to include notations on game path to indicate that the player has either lost a turn or earned an extra turn. See close-up game board photo for ideas on the Geometry Curse board game. Scan and enlarge the photo for a closer look.

9. Children will roll the dice after they have correctly answered a problem card. They lose their turn if they answer incorrectly.

Offer a small prize or raffle ticket to the child who wins the board game.

Flash Card Terror: For this game, you will have an electronic dinosaur serve as the timer. Your child must answer the question before the dinosaur reaches them. Time it so that it takes about 5 seconds for the dinosaur to get to your child.

Write out questions on index cards to make flash cards. For example, you might questions your child as follows:

- What is the number for pi?
- What is a line that goes from the center to the outside of a circle called?
- What is the formula for the area of a circle?
- What is the line that goes all the way across a circle called?
- What is the formula for the perimeter of a circle?

Be sure and write the correct answer on the back of the cards. You may want to let students self-practice with the cards before the game begins.

Sit a student on the floor on a predetermined spot. Place dinosaur far enough away that it takes about five seconds for him to reach his victim when he is moving forward. Have an additional Teacher Helper available to work dinosaur. Student must provide the correct answer to the flash card before dinosaur reaches him in order to move on to the next card or game.

I suggest you have 4-5 flash cards and students keep taking alternating turns until they have answered all cards correctly. It is expected that students will move their bodies to avoid dinosaur capture. If electronic dinosaur catches you, you lose a turn.

Whenever a student is able to avoid dinosaur capture and answer all five cards correctly, they are rewarded by being allowed to race a remote control car or helicopter (or whatever remote control vehicle you have available) around dinosaur three times and given a raffle ticket.

Mold glitter pipe cleaners into a head dress for the girls. The curve at the front forms a snake.

After-Party

Provide refreshments and give-away academic prizes at this time.

Air Gun Arcade: (Prepare arcade before children arrive so it can serve as an incentive for them to do the hard academic work.) Stack three baskets or crates pyramid-style to create

Achieving Brilliance at Home

levels. Cover with sand-colored fabric.

Cover large (posable and trashable) action figures in gauze bandage fabric to resemble mummies and stand on levels.

The mummies will be the targets for the air gun gun arcade. Alternatively, you may use large plastic dinosaurs as arcade targets.

An air gun with a sight works much better for this purpose, but use your own discretion in determining what will be the most fun and the safest for your children.

Photo Set-Up (See photo at chapter heading.)

1. On a piece of white poster board, affix two silhouettes that resemble jackals and give them glitter eyes.

2. Use large leaf shapes to decorate corners of poster board if desired.

3. Male headpiece (shown in photo at chapter heading) is made from 2-3 bright blue pieces of heavier weight construction paper taped lengthwise. Leave one side of the headpiece open so it can lay out flat. Decorate with glitter, allow to dry overnight, measure to the size you want and tape. I was surprised to discover that the construction paper would indeed stand up lengthwise even with all of the heavy glitter.

4. Female headpiece is fashioned from gold glitter pipe cleaners and the front is shaped into snake form. You will need to work with this form to determine adequate sizing needs, placement on head and height of snake decoration in front. A girl can wear the same chest decoration (described below) as a boy.

5. For the chest decoration, measure and cut out a neckline in a piece of construction paper lengthwise. Hole punch each shoulder and thread twirling ribbons through to knot so that they allow the chest piece to go over the head and hang from

> the shoulders when worn.
>
> 6. Take digital photos of your attendees and encourage them to sign up the next math session so you can have their photos available for them.
>
> The next time you're in the Atlanta area, visit the Michael Carlos Museum at Emory University to see real Egyptian mummies.

Achieving Brilliance at Home

Alien Sock Hop & Martian Measurement

Pretend your space craft has fallen through a tear in time and landed in you in 1950's America. Then, imagine aliens really did invade the Earth. Now, imagine they turned out to be friendly and fun!

Pre-Event	Costume	After Party	Arcade & Photos
Determine Location	Soda Jerk hat, white button shirt and black bow tie	1950's Sock Hop Music	Three baskets for stacking
Flyers & Posters	Blue straight-leg jeans, penny loafers, white socks, white plain t-shirt with sleeves cuffed, slick back hair with gel, black leather jacket	Ice Cream, Malted Powder and Root Beer	Air gun with light pointer
Sign-In Sheet			
Money Handler	Pony tail tied with scarf, poodle skirt (pin paper poodle to regular full skirt and use ribbon for leash), pink, black & white colors, white socks, saddle shoes if available.	Cups, Napkins, Bowls, spoons,	Green blow-up aliens
Helper Teachers		1950's decorations, posters, 45 rpm records, etc.	Give away prizes
Take Home Cards	Any 1950's style dress	Candy, popcorn	Digital Camera

153

Games & Activities Supplies

Math Textbook

Celsius/Fahrenheit Thermometer

Mini-silhouettes of pints, gallons, quarts bottles, made on three (3) colors of construction paper

Coat, jacket, swim suit/trunks, t-shirt (as regards appropriate dress for the weather)

Salt & water to make salt dough:
1 cup salt
1 cup all purpose flour,
1 cup luke warm water

Graph paper,

A well-known silly surgery game,

Time clock (kindergarten clock with moveable hands)

Time zone map

Deciliter, liter, grams, kiloliter, centimeter, meter, kilometer containers

Gallon, quart, pint, cup, ½, 1/3, ¼, measuring containers and measuring spoons

Inch, foot, yard, mile = ruler, yard stick

Ton, pound, ounces = scale

Gram, kilogram, metric ton = metric scale

Dry erase markers

Dry erase sheets

Games & Activities

Math Textbook: Use the examples from the front of the lesson in the textbook to create your problems. Be sure and show the steps you took to solve a problem on your answer key for your Teacher Helper. You will use the textbook to reinforce session learning during the following week through homework and/or worksheets that you create. If your child is still having trouble, just repeat the session until they get it. Do not change the problems in the session until your child is clear on the process for solving the problem.

Celsius/Fahrenheit Thermometer: Lay out a large thermometer which shows both Celsius and Fahrenheit and review that we use Fahrenheit in America and that, overseas, they use Celsius. Create a Celsius/Fahrenheit thermometer as shown in the following photo to make it more fun and memorable.

I've provided sample playing cards after the photos to help your students quickly familiarize themselves with the basic idea of the difference in temperatures between Fahrenheit and Celsius.

My little alien slides up and down. If your students aren't getting it, you may want to lay out a coat, a sweater or jacket, a t-shirt and a swimsuit/swim trunks. Have your student pick up the appropriate article of clothing to solidify the idea in their minds.
Alternatively, you may want to make paper clothes (like a paper doll) for your child to put on the alien.

The formula is provided as additional information only.

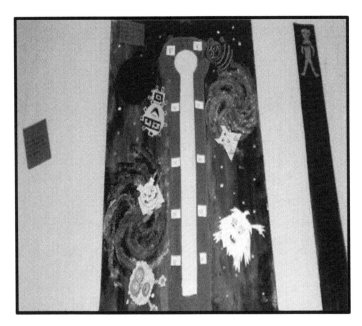
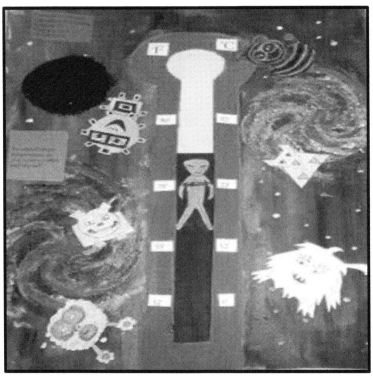

Achieving Brilliance at Home

At what Celsius temperature do you wear a jacket?	At what Celsius temperature do you wear a swim suit or trunks?	Formula to convert <u>Fahrenheit to Celsius:</u> Subtract 32 Multiply by 5 Divide by 9
At what Fahrenheit temperature do you wear a jacket?	At what Fahrenheit temperature do you wear a swim suit or trunks?	
At what Celsius temperature do you wear a coat?	At what Celsius temperature do you wear a t-shirt and shorts?	
At what Fahrenheit temperature do you wear a coat?	At what Fahrenheit temperature do you wear a t-shirt and shorts?	(*Hint:* Create a table to make your playing cars.)

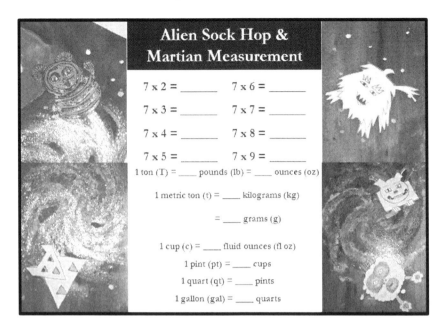

Take Home Card: Always give your child a take-home/bulletin board card to help them remember what they learned at your sessions. Select whatever information you would like to reinforce to appear on the card. They can attach the card to their bulletin board at home and then reinforce what they learned by showing it to their family and friends and telling them about it.

Martian Measurement: Mars uses the metric system so it's very important that you child gets a feel for how it compares to the system we use in the United States. Label multiple containers with both standard and metric measurements to help children see how they compare. Have Teacher Helper request children provide her Helper with given quantities of rice. Use a funnel to make it easier to pour the rice into the smaller-necked containers. You may want to place this learning center on a large sheet of paper to make for easier clean-up..

Thirsty Refresher: Cut out multiple sets of miniature pints, quarts and gallons as shown above. Have children lay out pieces as shown above. Then, children will tell Teacher Help what they done. Finally, Teacher Helper will ask them questions such as "How many pints are in a gallon?" "How many pints are in two quarts?" Have child come up with their own combination if they're having fun.

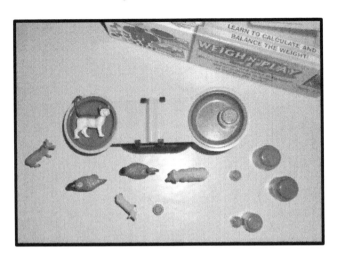

Mini-Martian Animals: On Mars, they have all the same animals that we do (*except that they are miniature*). See the previous two photos. Have your child weigh several Martian animals using mini plastic animal figures and a Weigh N'Play set. After they get the idea, see if they can guesstimate the number of grams a given animal will weigh.

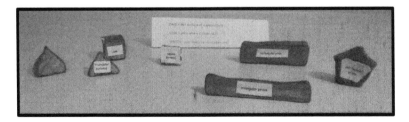

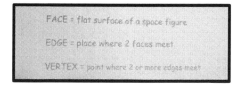

Martian Bird's Eggs: Make these "eggs" out of salt dough (recipe follows) and shape them into shapes that fit your needs. I painted the "eggs" neon green and ran and line of neon red paint along the edges to make them easier to see. Have students count the number of faces, edges and vertices. Go over how the shapes are named by their bases such as a triangular base for a triangular pyramid, etc. Have students find shapes and tell Teacher Helper how their base relates to their name.

Salt Dough Recipe follows.

Salt Dough Recipe:

1 cup salt
1 cup all purpose flour,
1 cup luke warm water

Mix all into a dough texture and use to create "Alien Bird's Eggs." Allow to dry for a few days (or even a week) before painting.

Rather than making your child wait for the eggs to dry, you may want to go ahead and make them yourself completely. Print and cut out the names of the shapes you have made. Have your child simply glue the name to the correct egg.

Time Zone Take-Off: Lay out a time zone map (easy to find on the internet) and a toy clock with moveable hands (you may have to go to a school supply site for this clock). Make up travel cards that detail a trip from Atlanta to Los Angeles, for example. Provide the number of travel hours (around 4) required for the trip. Create problem cards along the lines of, "If you left Atlanta at 9:00 a.m., what time would it be when you got to Los Angeles?"

Answer key: If the trip takes 4 hours and Los Angeles is about 3 hours behind Atlanta (based on the time zone map), it will be 10:00 a.m. Make several of these game cards to go over with your students before actual play begins. Remember, the point is to solidify in your child's mind what they need to do in order to calculate the difference in time zones (not perform excruciating math work).

Alien Astronaut Probe: Oh, no, it looks like our astronaut is being examined by the aliens. Don't worry, he turns out to be just fine in the end. Their advanced technology enables them to examine our astronaut without hurting him. What a relief!

Achieving Brilliance at Home

Pass out silly surgery games body parts for which students can figure out the area as shown on the instruction card that follows.

1. Draw your body part figure on plain white paper.
2. Cut it out.
3. Cut it apart to cover as many squares below as fully as possible.
4. Tell how squares it covers mostly. That is the AREA.
5. Put the figure in the right | silly surgery | slot.
6. During the party, you can try to get your figure out Without setting off the buzzer.

Good Luck!

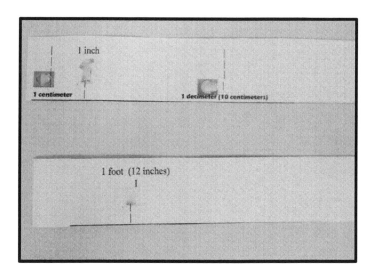

1 centimeter   1 inch   1 decimeter (10 centimeters)

1 foot (12 inches)

Martian Stretch: Cut apart a sheet of card stock and mark with standard and metric measurement so students can compare. Have them make special note of how long a meter is compared to a yard stick. Have them find something in the room that is close to a yard long and something that is close to a meter long. See examples or word problems in your math textbook for ideas of items that students can measure.

After-Party: Play 1950's music for your after party. Have a Soda Jerk (see costumes) serve ice cream sodas and teach your child how to do the Swing. The basic steps are as follows:

The 1950's Swing

Boy always start on their left foot and girls always start on their right foot.

The boy has his right hand on the girl's waist and his left arm is extended and holds the girl's right hand.

The girl has her left hand on the boy's right shoulder and her right arm is extended and her hand is resting in boy's hand.

Begin with feet together and the boy will lead.

Boys lightly stomps three times to the left, lightly stomps three times to the right and, then, boy rocks back on his left foot and girl rocks back on her right foot one time (rocking *away* from each other).

Repeat. (Do everything in slow motion when learning and learn and practice the dance yourself before attempting to teach it to your child.)

Look on YouTube for "1950's Swing" to find several examples of turns and additional moves you can do as part of the fun. If you have access to a television during your learning session, it would be great to show these moves so the kids can dance them with the dancers for fun. If they don't want to dance as couples, they could just perform the tricks shown on the video by themself.

Any space, alien or 1950's themed decorations are fine as regards prizes, raffle give-aways and arcade figures.

Air gun Arcade: Plastic aliens work well (but wear goggles in case the air darts bounce back off of the plastic) for purpose of example in this book. You want to set up three baskets or crates to create a pyramid and then cover it in (neon green?) cloth. Ideally, you would set up three plastic aliens on the levels. Wear eye goggles as the air darts may bounce back off of the plastic aliens.

Another option is to base it on the 1950's and use any kind of blow-up found at a party store. Safety Note: Your students (and you) will need to use goggles if you use balloons or blow-ups for the air gun arcade as the rubber nosed air bullets tend to bounce back and you will want to make sure that everyone's eyes are protected. Test a few before you actually do the arcade to see how far your bullets bounce back.

Last Amazon Tribe & Probability and Statistics

The simple story line for this theme could be that the rain forests are being cut down and these primitive tribes are becoming endangered through threats from the outside world. (Actually, the abuse of these people has become very bad due to loggers.) We all need to help protect these people from our global society.

Achieving Brilliance at Home

Pre-Event	Snacks	Games & Activities	After-Party
Determine Location	Cupcakes	Math Textbook	3 baskets for stacking
Flyers & Posters	Drinks	Bingo Spinner /raffle drum	3-5 plastic tropical fruit drink cups with the straws removed (tape or glue sections together and wear eye goggles)
Sign-In Sheet	Cups	Wooden blocks	
	Napkins	Card stock and construction paper	
Money Handler	Plates		
	Candy	Crayons	
Helper Teachers	Dark Green Tablecloth	Colored Markers	Air gun with light pointer
		Twirling Ribbon	
Take Home Cards		Coat Hangar	Give away prizes
		Tree Illustration	
		Boy and Girl Flip-Side Cards	Digital Camera
		Dice	
		Amazon Props such as a snake.	

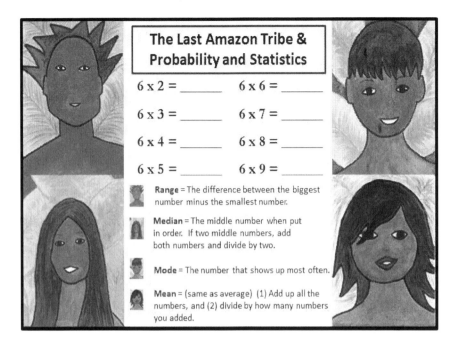

Take-Home Card: Always make take-home cards for your attendees to take home and show to their parents. Your child can post his bulletin board card in his room (where he will look at it occasionally over time and this will serve as a review).

Please note that all games and activities were created by following the lessons of the math textbook I used when I created them. Use the lesson examples from your own textbook to create personalized materials based on your child's learning preferences and learning needs. The lesson for you to learn is to be blatant in adapting materials to the needs of your child so that he can learn easily.

That said, it is not unusual for you to create a game that your child immediately masters and then you say to yourself, "It took me two hours to think up and make up this game and he mastered it in 10 minutes." Congratulations, you made up a great learning game.

Achieving Brilliance at Home

If you have any doubts as to whether it was worth your time, money and energy, try to only put extra effort into creating additional materials when your child is struggling.

It is not uncommon for your child to be having a very difficult and frustrating time learning an idea only to discover that they can understand the material within a few minutes using a multisensory and fun approach. Just make sure they can transfer the information they learned to practice exercises from their textbook and/or worksheets. As they do their worksheets, they can now visualize the memorable game in their mind.

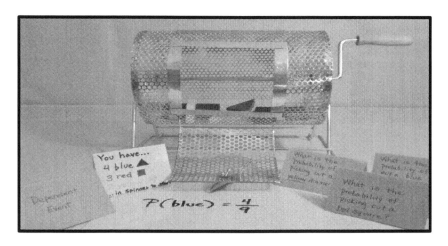

Block Spin: Put colored wooden blocks in a Bingo spinner or a raffle drum to help your student understand how to write out a probability (on a dry erase sheet) and answer the questions asked on your game cards. The Dependent Event is where your students removes one block after they spin, selects a problem, and then determines the new probability.

Most of the games and activities for this and the next unit were created by hand. For this book, it was necessary to create all of the illustrations myself (or get special permission) to avoid copyright infringement issues. For your purposes, simply print pictures and illustrations off of the internet or buy used books at a thrift shop and cut out the pictures to use for illustrations.

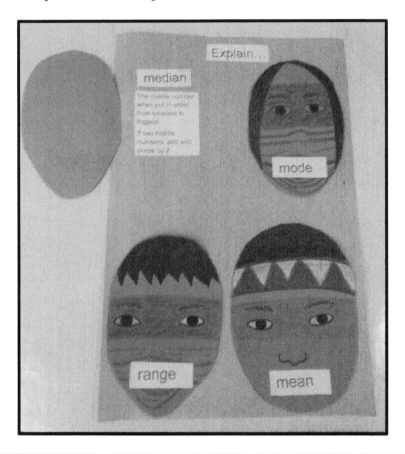

Amazon Warrior Flash Cards: Create memorable flash cards for important information. Faces open like booklets to reveal the answer beneath. Quiz your child as you would for flash cards. Lightly tap a pencil slowly three times and encourage your child to begin answering before the third tap.

If your child is really having trouble, have them read the answer and then ask them the same question again (several times if necessary) until they can remember it.

Achieving Brilliance at Home

If your child is still having trouble, let them learn one a day. The second day, you will ask them the first question and then add the second (if they can do it successfully). You will do this daily for four days. On the fifth day, they may well be able to say them all easily.

If they are still truly struggling and starting to lose confidence, you will ask them the same question every day until *they* realize that they have learned the information.

Let them enjoy the feeling of success and reinforce that feeling by always reviewing what they have now successfully learned before proceeding with new information.

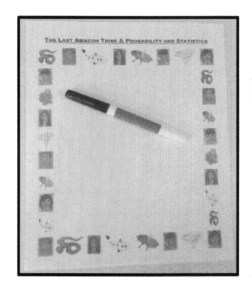

Use themed border paper to create a dry erase sheet by placing it in a plastic report cover with the spine removed. If possible, do this for all of the unit themes to maintain the novelty of using the dry erase sheet.

Jeanne Mifflin

Fruit Picked by the Amazon Tribe Children: Create game cards using simple depictions of fruit. Write varying numbers in the lower right-hand corner of each card that your student will use to average the amount of fruit picked per day. I suggest you let your student "draw" five cards from a bag or basket themselves. They will then use the dry erase sheet and marker to figure out the answer.

Keep the numbers low and easy. The point is to help them remember how to find an average as opposed to truly practicing the skill.

Intensive practice can be done during the week using math textbook-assigned homework or worksheets.

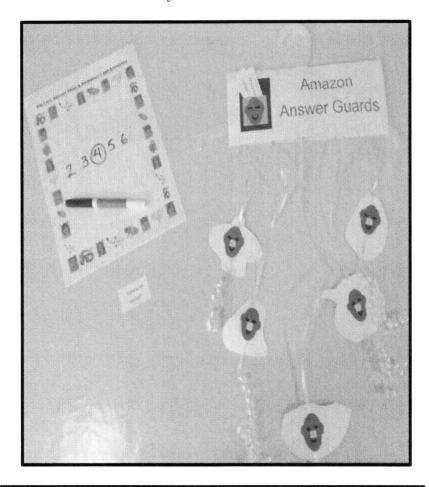

Amazon Answer Guards Hanging Mobile: To find mean, median and mode, createe question cards (with the correct answer written on the back) and tuck them into a pocket at the top of the mobile. The numbers the children will use to answer the questions are written on the back of the animal illustrations. The children will use the dry erase sheet and marker to figure out the correct answer. Try hanging the mobile but, if your child gets frustrated turning the pictures, lay it flat on a table to make it easier to manipulate. Some children really enjoy chasing the backs of the pictures and some really do not. Use your good judgment.

Achieving Brilliance at Home

Tree Diagram: You will need two two-sided cards. The boy card has a picture of the boy on both sides. The girl card has a picture of the girl on both sides. Paste (corners only) a strip of clear plastic report cover over the bottom of the picture on which your child can write out their tree diagrams. Your child can either draw the cards from a sack or you can simply explain. If your picture is important to you, you will want to laminate it or be very careful not to smear the marker on your picture when you are cleaning the dry erase portion.

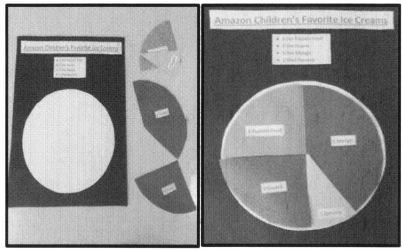

Game Set-Up   Completed Game

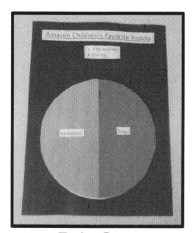

Easier Game

Amazon Pie Charts: Come up with something fun that your child likes and create sections of a pie chart. The idea is to give them something to handle and to get them in the habit of looking for a legend and relating that to the pie. The previous example used a total of ten students. *Special Note*: Novelty is the key to fun in learning. If you have a wood puzzle substitution available, use it. Just be sure and create a theme-related aspect to it so that it once again becomes "new."

If your child is really having trouble with the concept, create an extremely simple example (such as the two halves shown in the previous illustration). Point to and read the heading and legend. Point to and read pie pieces and place them on the game sheet. Take the pieces off and have your student "pretend" to do exactly the same thing you did. After a couple of times, surprise, they actually start to understand what they are doing.

Additionally, gather 10 human or animal figures and line them up. Place two pieces of real fruit (and use the same fruit names on your graph) on the table and sort the figures into the two fruits. Then, place your construction paper pie pieces next to the appropriate group or stand the figures on their pie piece as you count them out. Finally, transfer the pie piece to the game sheet. Have your student "pretend to learn" by imitating you (or you putting your hands on top of theirs and gently guiding them through the procedure).

The child thinks that they're fooling you and they have no intention of learning anything. Go along and pretend you don't know. Guess what? They learned.

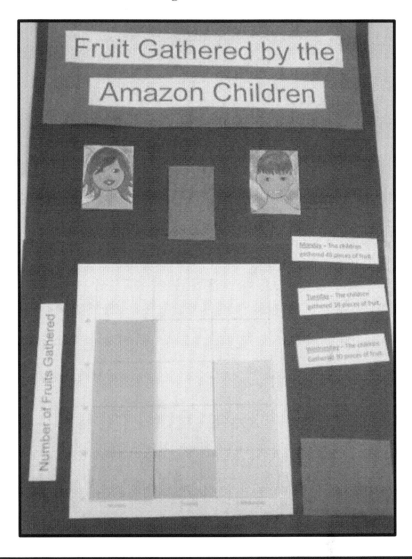

Amount of Fruit Gathered by the Amazon Children: To help your child learn to read bar charts, create a quick and easy game that teaches them to read the appropriate axis for information. Prepared construction paper bars are tucked into a pocket on the right and question cards are housed in the small top pocket.

Jeanne Mifflin

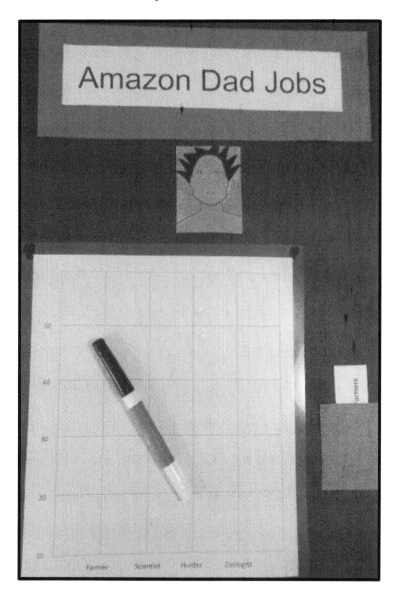

Completed Game

Amazon Dad Jobs: Set-up your game sheet using a computer-prepared graph with a piece of plastic report covered affixed over the top. Question cards are placed in a pocket to the right of the graph until needed. Your child will place dots at the appropriate point on the graph using a dry erase marker and then connect them to make a line graph.

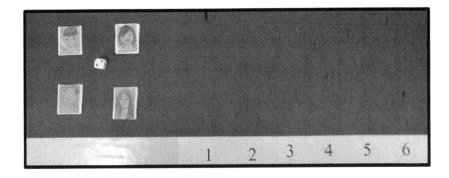

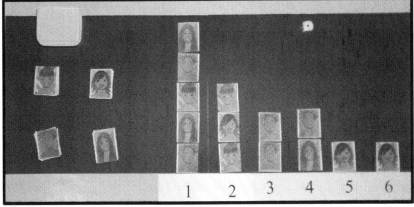

Completed Game

Strange Coincidences Game: (See game set up shown previously.) Pulling game cards from left to right and top to bottom, have you child roll a dice and place a game card over the appropriate number. Create about 10 cards for each character.

Continue until one number column reaches the top of the game sheet. Look at the surprising results for this game of chance. Were all the cards distributed evenly? Were there numbers that a character hit on more than once? Play the game three times to see how the results differ.

Achieving Brilliance at Home

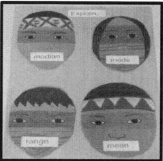

After-Party and Photo Opportunity: The men in the last Amazon tribe found red face paint to cover their faces. Create paper plate face masks, paint them red and staple elastic to the undersides to run across the back of your child's head to keep them on your student's face. Alternatively, your student may want to paint their faces with clown face paint to resemble the Amazonians. Several different tribes are depicted above. I don't recommend using face paint around a child's eyes and would prefer you use a woman's eye shadow instead.

Your photo backdrop will consist of green construction paper cut to resemble palm leaves and affixed to a sky blue backdrop so that they hang over forward from their midpoint. Crushed green tissue paper can serve as additional tree-like greenery. Brown paper crushed and twisted serves as your tree trunk and hanging vines, if desired. You may want to hang stuffed animal monkeys, snakes, etc., from your vines like we did for an international community play room we held at the local community center.

(See photos that follow.)

Jeanne Mifflin

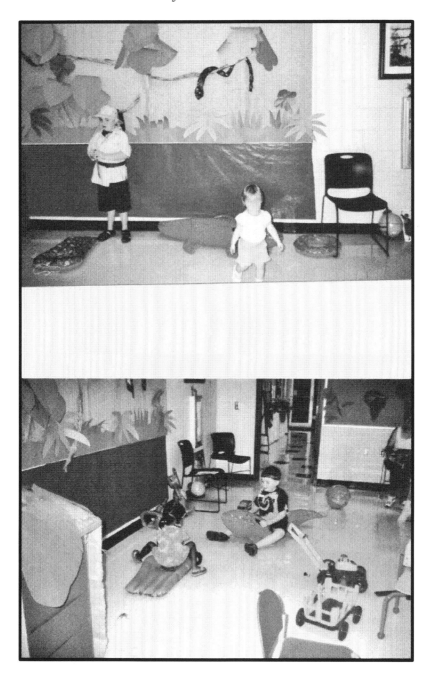

Achieving Brilliance at Home

Greek Mythology & The Hercules Fraction Flip

Simply go over a nonfiction book on Greek mythology for this theme instead of trying to come up with a story line. The stories are so dazzling in themselves that no further embellishment is needed. Find a good classic movie to complement the theme for even more fun.

Pre-Event	Snacks	After-Party
Determine Location	Grapes and Other Fruits	3 baskets for stacking
Flyers & Posters	Drinks	3-5 "Lightning Bolts" formed from aluminum foil
Sign-In Sheet	Cups	3-5 evil mythical stand-up card figures to serve as targets
	Napkins	
Money Handler	Plates	Air gun with light pointer
	Candy or	A white sheet wrapped into the form of a toga and a headpiece of

Pre-Event	Snacks	After-Party
	Cupcakes	leaves serve as the costume.
Helper Teachers	White tablecloth	You may want to add a stone necklace for girls.
Take Home Cards		Give away prizes
		Digital Camera

Greek Mythology & The Hercules Fraction Flip Take-Home Card: Be sure and make take-home cards for your students to place on the bulletin board in their room to help them remember the session. I always liked to use them to help your student practice their multiplication facts as well.

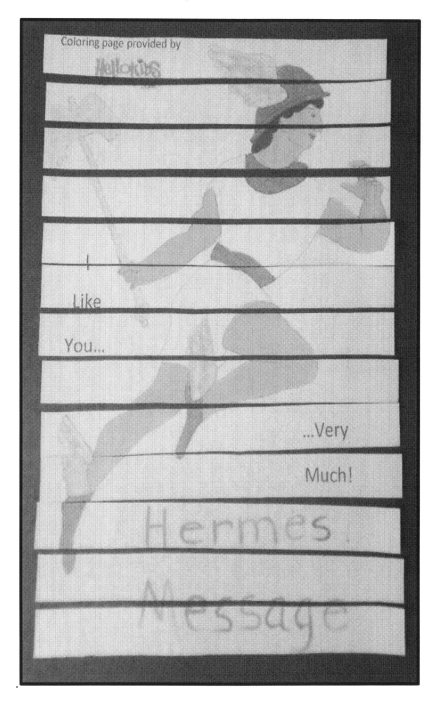

Jeanne Mifflin

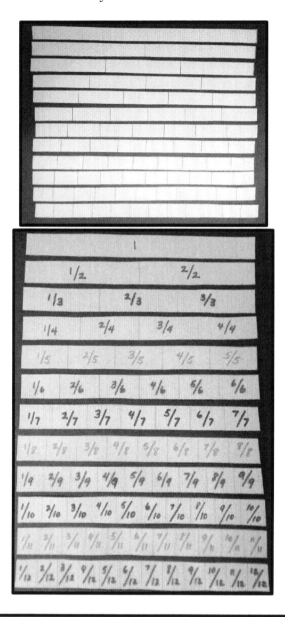

Hermes Message: To help your child grasp the concept of equivalent fractions, print a picture onto white card stock of Hermes from the internet or create one of your own using the coloring pages at HelloKids.com. Create a table and break the rows down into fraction cells. See the answer key to guide you in the number of cells you will need for each row. Print the table onto the back of a Hermes picture.

Cut apart the rows and give them to your child advising them to write out their fractions as shown on the answer key. After all rows have been completed, line them up from 1 to 1/12 as shown in photo. Flip answer rows over to read Hermes Message. For more practice, you may want to have your child color a specific amount on their row (5/8, for example) with a colored pencil to firmly establish this concept in their mind.

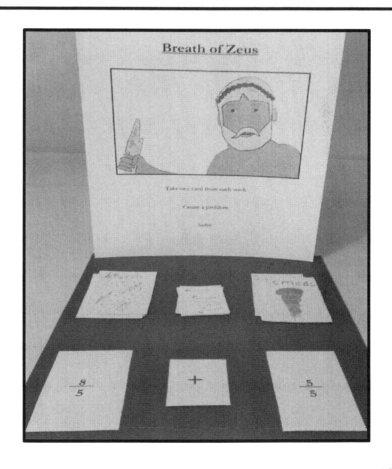

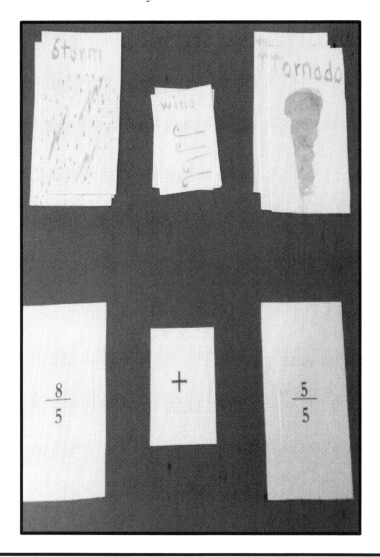

Breath of Zeus: This game is used to practice adding fractions with the same denominator. The trick, sometimes, is turning an improper fraction result into a mixed number. Have your student use a dry erase sheet and marker to figure out their answer if necessary. When creating your game cards, make sure that you have larger fractions on the left and smaller fractions on the right to avoid problems when your student pulls a subtraction card from the middle. I used fractions 10/5 through 6/5 on the left and 5/5 through 1/5 on the right.

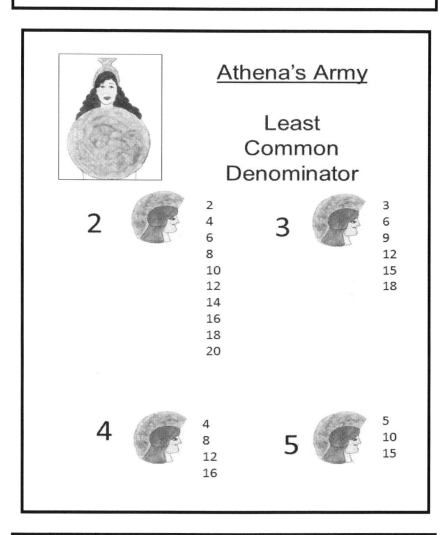

Athena's Army – Least Common Denominator: Have your student practice finding the least common denominator of some easy numbers like the ones shown above.

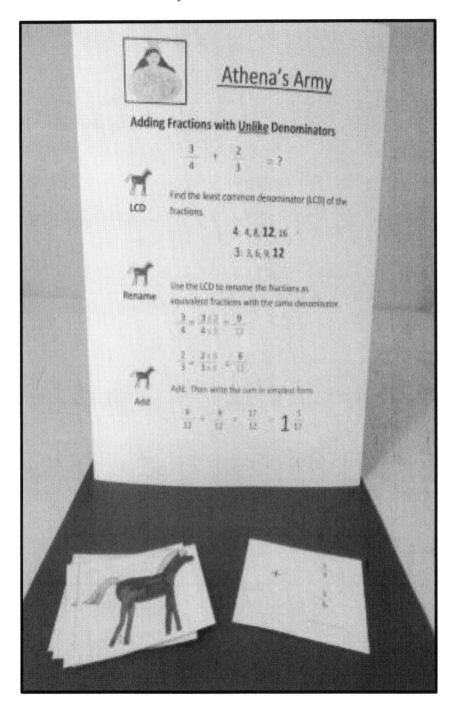

Achieving Brilliance at Home

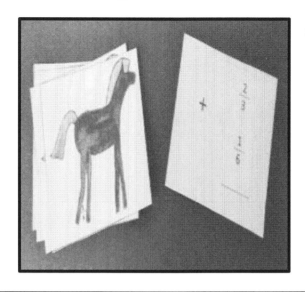

Athena's Army and Adding Fractions with Unlike Denominators: Create a standing card that reviews the procedure for adding two fractions with unlike denominators as shown in previous photos. Fold a full length of cardstock in a trifold and tape it to the back of your instructions card to get the card to stand up. Create playing cards with simple problems for your student to solve like the one shown above..

You may want to hide the answer on the outside of the playing card somewhere on or next to the pony. This will make it so much easier for you to check answers without scrambling to look for the answer sheet. Even though the students figure it out, it becomes part of the game to check their answer themselves. Just don't let them spend a lot of time memorizing the answer before they begin the problems. I like to hide my answers somewhere the students will be able to find them. It makes it part of the fun (like a treasure hunt)

Athena's Army

Adding Fractions with <u>Unlike</u> Denominators

$$\frac{3}{4} + \frac{2}{3} = ?$$

LCD

Find the least common denominator (LCD) of the fractions.

4: 4, 8, **12**, 16

3: 3, 6, 9, **12**

Rename

Use the LCD to rename the fractions as equivalent fractions with the same denominator.

$$\frac{3}{4} = \frac{3 \times 3}{4 \times 3} = \frac{9}{12}$$

$$\frac{2}{3} = \frac{2 \times 4}{3 \times 4} = \frac{8}{12}$$

Add

Add. Then write the sum in simplest form.

$$\frac{9}{12} + \frac{8}{12} = \frac{17}{12} = 1\frac{5}{12}$$

Achieving Brilliance at Home

Greek Bull's Eye: Use this game to help your child become comfortable with converting improper fractions into mixed numbers. Do a couple of these problems using a dry erase sheet before your start. Remember, the point is to take the fear out of doing these types of problems so please don't make them so challenging that they become frustrating. Let your student work up to harder problems. In the meantime, let them enjoy the feeling of easy success.

Eros Multiplying Fractions: Create an instruction sheet for your student, as shown above, and playing cards on which you've written various multiplication fraction problems. Have your student work out the problem on a dry erase sheet. If possible, hide the correct answer on the reverse side of the card to make it easier to keep moving. If your student starts to balk, wave your hand at the party area to remind them of the goodies that await.

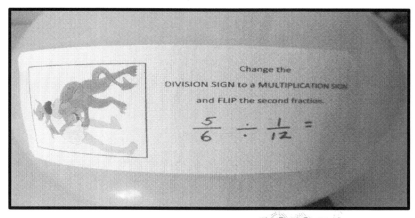

Coloring page provided by HelloKids

Hercules Fraction Flip: Create two signs indicating simple instructions for how to divide fractions and tape them to the opposite sides of a large ball. Depending on the ability of your child, you may want to stick to the simple instructions shown in the photo. Make an exact duplicate of your card except that the division sign is now multiplication and the second fraction is reversed. When your child spins or "flips" the ball, the multiplication card will be revealed from the other side. If you'd like to be more precise in your directions, try the following:

1. Multiply by the reciprocal of the divisor.

2. Cancel where possible.

3. Multiply the numerators and the denominators.

4. Rename if an improper fraction.

The simple rhyme shown below adds to the fun.

Who can tell me the Hercules Flip?
Who can tell me, "What is it?"

Bounce the ball on the floor and then toss it to your child. He will then (1) read out loud the first card, (2) throw the ball up in the air to switch signs, and (3) then read off the second sign.

After your child has a good idea of the procedure, have them practice a few division problems using the dry erase sheet.

Savannah, GA

VIII. Wings of Brilliance

Let's rediscover holidays, field trips and special events as a family event. Holidays seem to have become an academic event all instead of a family togetherness event through the years. Let's take them back.

Free Fun

From the time they are a toddler, you should get in the habit of taking your child to the park for an hour a day until they outgrow the playground setting (around 10).

The first week or so, take your child from activity to activity (slide to ladder, for instance) and, placing your hands on top of their's gently, show your child where to place their feet and hands and take them through the process of using the equipment. Write down the order that you do the tasks in so you can do it the same way each time.

Whenever possible, take your child to the park and walk them through the activities exactly the same way. Insist that they must do all of the activities before they can free play. It will take some work and consistent structure, but your child will get better and better at the equipment. Be sure and give them at least 20 minutes of free play after they've done all of your activities.

If you have a child that's reluctant to play on the equipment, try playing "Follow the Leader" with a child that has much better physical skills. You don't want a super athlete that presents an unattainable goal for your child, just a child who is more comfortable doing the activities and *enjoys* doing them and can show your child how much *fun* it is. Your child follows the other child through all the playground equipment and then the other child follows your child. Great fun for both!

"P.E. Central" is a great physical exercise resource. It is loaded with activities and games sorted by grade level, activity, holiday themes, etc., that make exercise fun. Some of the games are even appropriate for parties!

Scouting is a great social and self-discovery outlet. Boys usually have an opportunity to play physical games and play running games before/after the meetings. There is also an additional sports and academics program that gives your son a chance to gain sports skills while earning pins.

Clearly, if your son is athletic, you should enroll him in sports classes. Most counties offer sports classes at a reasonable price. You'll need to check and see what's available in your area.

Focus on the Library

The library is a favored outing. If you have behavior problems at the library, take a sheet of construction paper and fold into a booklet listing the rules for the library and what the rewards are for following the rules. This can easily be done on the computer in a cute font (and it always works best if you insert a picture of your child and the title, <u>My Library Rules</u>, on the front cover.)

Rules (when your child is learning to read) might include picking out 6-8 books and 2-3 videos and bringing them to the table. Then, your child has to read one of the books (or scan each page if it was a harder book) before they can play on the computer.

If your child becomes difficult during library story time, leave immediately so as not to reward them with library free play or computer time. Yes, they will be upset at first.

You may discover that your child finds it rewarding to check out their books using the library's electronic scanning system. Tgeur ability to do this depends on their behavior in the library.

Frequent Store Outings

If your child screams and tantrum in the store for toys, you must buy them nothing or you will be continually blackmailed for toys when people are looking. Try to be as stubborn as a frost in winter (even if it upsets store personnel). Once they start to behave, allow a turning to the positive.

A game that most children enjoy is to have their own "shopping list:" and they help locate (and weigh) the families groceries for the week.

Fabulous Holidays

Plan all holiday and summer activities. Even if you don't follow your plan exactly, it will keep your family running along smoothly despite the many disruptions and changes in routine.. Oddly, as much as your child may scream "unfair," they will do much better if their days are filled with some sort of planned activity.

If you think that TV and video games will do the trick, wait and watch the irritability set in -- go figure. You will always come out ahead if you can wear your child out without becoming completely exhausted yourself.

The worst plan is one in which Mom is exhausted the rest of the family is full of energy and bored. This is the scenario when Mom cleans the house, does the laundry, makes a big meal, cleans the kitchen, finally sits down to rest and the family announce that it's bored (and the implied threat that they are all going to tantrum if Mom doesn't come up with something fun to do). Smile warmly now.

Fanciful Party Ideas

Find a children's video that shows a full party. A TV dinosaur had a Halloween party video that was excellent for this purpose. Recreate all of the scenes, games, props, crafts, etc., for your own Halloween party. Your child will be so surprised and will truly love it if they are very familiar with the video.

Georgia Aquarium, Atlanta, GA

Field Trips

The following list should spark your creativity when looking for a great place to take your child for a field trips related to what you are trying to teach them.

- Scouts is a cornucopia of weekly fun activities and events,
- Dairy farms, zoos and petting farms,
- Free outdoor concerts and festivals
- Historic sites and reenactments,
- Home school conventions and expos
- Lessons of any type,
- Music Store
- Local home school club in your area.
- Mini-golf, laser tag, bowling, skating, swimming pool,
- Movies (especially the free movies during the summer at many theaters),
- Museums, symphony orchestras, ballet

- Planetariums, science centers and nature preserves,
- Sporting events,
- State parks and lakes, camping, canoeing, swimming, horseback riding,
- Summer camps (some offer scholarships -- check the one you're interested in)
- Theatre performances (especially if they relate to what you're studying), and
- Theme parks and local attractions (watch for specially priced home school day offerings).

Check online when you're planning a field trip to see if they offer special educational aids. For example, Zoo Atlanta offers free kits of specialized instructional materials, that you can reserve in advance, if you're a teacher or homeschooler. The Georgia Aquarium has coloring pages on their site.

Fun Ideas from Theme Parks

Think of the inexpensive activities that theme parks and hotels offer and recreate them in your back yard in order to help your child learn or even just for fun. Find inexpensive alternatives that offer the same experience in your area.

- Outdoor dining (picnics and barbeques in the back yard)
- Swimming pool with slides and fountains,
- Free fireworks,
- Parks and playgrounds,
- Mini-golf,
- White sand beaches (even if they're lake beaches),

Achieving Brilliance at Home

- Biking, fishing, paddle boating,

- Waterfalls,

- Archaeological Dig (in Georgia, go as far as your own backyard -- be sure and add a hammock for Dad),

- Log Cabins, camping, hiking, cave and gold mine exploring, tubing, horseback riding, canoeing, campfires, sing-alongs (North Georgia is loaded with these types of experiences not to mention camping), and

- Beach experiences (Tybee Island, by Savannah, is a nice secluded family-friendly beach and the Tybee Island Marine Science Center puts on quite the show during the animal's feeding time).

- Buy an annual pass for theme parks, like our Stone Mountain Park, if you live in the area. If you can't afford the attractions pass, a parking pass may get you in where you and your child can still enjoy the playground, water features and take strolls through the main area, and possibly other amenities.. At Stone Mountain Park, little kids love to play in the water stream in front of the restaurant (for free).

- Circus and animal parks and petting zoos,

- Falcons and Braves games and other sports events,

- Amtrak or other train excursions,

- Chuck E Cheese for younger kids and Stars and Strikes for older elementary-aged kids,

- Specialty restaurants (especially as you are studying the country from which the restaurant food is derived),

- Small airports to watch the planes take off and land – (Gilmer in Gainesville and Peachtree DeKalb in Norcross), and

- North Georgia College offers free planetarium and observatory shows at different times throughout the year.

Research your own local attractions. Sometimes, if you go to a pool the last hour of the day, for example, there are special pricing breaks. Seasonal passes typically offer good discounts as well.

Preparing for K12 Fish Dissection Lesson

IX. Family of Brilliance

Never pull your child out of school as an act of spite against the school system. Be sure you are ready and able to do what it takes if you decide to home school. If home school isn't working, take your child back to school sooner rather than later.

The only rational reasons to home school are if your child is:

- Tumbling backward academically instead of progressing,
- Being babysat instead of being taught in school,
- Experiencing a teacher who has a bias against them (racial, economic status, religious, etc.),
- Coming home with large bruises or other injuries and/or complains of being bullied,

- Suffering exposure to evil influences, such as drugs and alcohol (and they are slowly infiltrating your child's life when they are at school), and
- You are prepared to do whatever it takes to educate them.

Is Homeschooling an Option?

The number one requirement for home schooling, in my opinion, is that you be a stay-at-home mother who is able to devote her entire day to the schooling of her child(ren).

That means that your husband must provide for the family entirely on his own. Don't plan on getting any chores done during school time (but you can get chores done if you have a structured system in place with the children for after-school time).

You'll be lucky to have three meals on the table and you will need to preplan activities for your children to work on while you cook. Never leave your child(ren) sitting with nothing to do during school time as they *will* get into trouble. Have a readymade list of activities they can do for those times when you won't be able to give them specific instructions (such as when an important call comes in unexpectedly or there's a knock at the door).

> **Never Leave Your Child Sitting With Nothing To Do**

You will, also, not be able to do child care for others and home school your child to a high standard. If you have children of your own that are several different ages, for each child's developmental age, your difficulty level will increase unless the older children can school the younger ones (and, even then, the older children are missing out on their own educational time). **You will have to be a master at planning, organization and preparation in order to succeed with multiple children of different ages and at different developmental levels.**

The following quiz will help you assess whether or not you are well suited to home schooling. They are issues that are typically addressed for teachers and will reveal how well-suited you currently are (as a parent) to the task of home schooling.

Attitude Aspirations	Good Answer	Bad Answer
I set the highest standards for myself and I'm willing to do whatever it takes for mastery.	If I can't offer my children something *better* than what they were getting in school, then why would I be home schooling?	They don't need to be that educated. They're breaking into show business and other people will take care of them.
I wake up at the same time every day and have the kids up, dressed, fed and we are all ready to start school by 8:00 a.m.	It may take a little practice, but I'm confident that I can ease into this type of structure given a few weeks.	We prefer to wake up around 10:00 a.m., have breakfast at 11:00 a.m., do one subject, break for lunch and then do the rest over the course of the day (unless we have a field trip).
I can tell you my child's likes and dislikes and what things they value so much that they are willing to work (very hard) to get them.	I never really thought about that much. I'll make notes over the next few days and see what I can come up with.	I'll just use whatever I can find at the store that's cheap. I'm not sure my child needs this. I'll just tell them what to do and they'll do it.

Attitude Aspirations	Good Answer	Bad Answer
I am well aware of what children should be learning at each age and grade.	I'm not sure what my child should be learning, but I will go to my state's Department of Education web site to find out and design my program around the specified goals. OR I am planning to purchase a full curriculum for my child.	I believe in no schooling. They'll let me know what they want to learn about through their interests.
My curriculum contains both academic and religious teachings.	Even though our faith is what's most important to me, in our society, children are expected to learn a full curriculum.	It's a competitive world so all we really care about is sports (so he can get a scholarship) and very basic academics.
I have a small library of books containing fun ideas for teaching, holiday themes, basic subject textbooks, a children's dictionary and thesaurus, incentive and behavior management ideas,	Wow, that's a lot of money. Let me see what I can find at thrift stores (even if they're a little dated) or at Amazon used. Maybe I'll swing into a school supply store so I'll know what types of things I'm looking for and see	I'll just use what I already have and can find at the library or discount store.

Attitude Aspirations	Good Answer	Bad Answer
and a comprehensive teacher text on reading instruction and another for math.	if they have anything affordable. OR We have the money right now so I'll just go to the school store and amazon online and save myself a lot of time and effort.	
My classroom is safe, clean and organized and the children's needs have been considered.	Let's see, I can use the basement (or kitchen in a pinch) if I move all the storage out. It should be safe as long as my walkways are clear, etc. I'll get some shelves for my supplies and move the computer down there. We have that extra children's table and chair set Aunt Martha gave us.	They can just do the work in their bedrooms.
I use songs, poems, fun activities and other ideas to make learning fun. If I can't find what I need, *I just make up a game or song myself.*	I can use the songs and games from TV shows, children's music CD's, and computer games to start. I'm not sure if I can do it all, but I'm willing to try.	I'll just tell them what they need to know and they'll learn it that way.

Attitude Aspirations	Good Answer	Bad Answer
If I notice that my child is not performing well, I will do a spot check of their physical health and react appropriately.	Even though I have put time and effort into preparing this lesson for my child, right now, it's more important to be a mom.	It's going to mess up our entire schedule if we don't get this lesson done today. They're just going to have to do it anyway.
I have planned rules and consequences and examples I can show my child of what I expect them to do.	Oh, I get it. I figure out the rules and consequences *beforehand* and make, or find, models (where appropriate) *beforehand* of specific assignments. I review all of my lessons *before* I do them with my child to make sure I have everything I need.	We'll just figure it out as we go along. I'm already putting in a lot of my time just getting everything pulled together.

Home School Mother's Promise to Herself

I realize that, at any point in time, it may be unexpectedly necessary for me to enroll my child in public school. For that reason, it's very important that my child is at the same grade level as their peers. (This mainly applies to a child who may be falling behind.)

It is important to keep our public school options open in case our family suffers a major setback. My child will suffer if I can't teach them and I won't let their education slip out of hand. I will take my child back to public school if we start to get into trouble.

You may be starting to figure out that this is going to be quite the adventure if you plan to do it well. I'm asking you to hold yourself up to high standards. If you do that, you will never be able to attain those high standards but you will go a lot higher than you would have with no or low standards.

Find a question to ask yourself that you find highly motivational during the rough times. I had the privilege of watching a top-notch special education teacher when my son was four. To this day, I picture her and try to imagine what she would do in a specific situation. Prayer is also a very powerful tool in clearing mental confusion as it helps you re-establish your true priorities.

If your child has been having great difficulties in a school setting, you can also look at it as putting all the time, money and energy you would have put into gas (to go to the school when your child has a problem), supplemental materials (to help your child learn what they are not learning at school, but are being taught) and preparation for IEP meetings, conferences, behavior modification planning, etc., into actually teaching your child. Even if you do have behavior issues that need to be addressed, you're only expending the emotional energy you would have in dealing with your child's behavior problems at school.

What are My Legal Requirements?

Declaration of Intent to Utilize a Home Study Program

In Georgia, you contact your county Board of Education and request that a "Declaration of Intent to Utilize a Home Study Program" and monthly attendance reporting forms be sent to your home (preferably a few weeks before you begin home schooling).
Complete the "Declaration..." form and return it as per the instructions provided.

Show your home school year as running for an *entire* year. If there is some kind of problem whereby you miss several weeks of school, you can still complete the mandatory number of school days required by your state during the specified school year by having it run through the summer.

The web site, www.hslda.org, provides home school regulation for each state and you may want to begin your information gathering there.

Monthly Attendance Reporting and Forms

After you receive your monthly attendance reporting forms, make one copy and fill in all of the information that will not be changing for that school year such as grade, name, address, school year beginning and ending dates, etc. Leave the line for the month and the boxes for the days empty. Make at least 12 copies (a couple of extras for mistakes). After you've made your copies with the unchanging information completed, use a brightly-colored marker to fill in the month.

Use a sheet protector turned sideways as a pocket and hang it in a prominent place. Insert the 12 copies of the attendance forms so that the current month faces out. This will serve as a daily reminder to turn in your forms. In Georgia, for example, you only have 15 days after the month ends to send in your forms.

At the beginning of each school year, buy a book of special stamps to be used only for attendance reporting and slip them into the sheet protector so that they show from the outside. Print out 12 pre-addressed envelopes (unless you expect the reporting address to change), showing my return name and address as well as the school system's Home School Department contact name and address, on the computer and stuff them in the back of the sheet protector.

The monthly attendance forms can go tricky quickly. Note all doctor's appointments, field trips, illness days, etc., on your regular family calendar. Make it your routine to have school daily during the week unless there is a special event or appointment planned and, even then, you can often make up school later in the day. At the end of the month, review your calendar and fill in the attendance reporting form.

I suggest you place an index card showing the month and the number of days reported for each month in the front of the sheet protector to maintain a running tally of your completed school days as compared to the required number of school days.

How Do I Put Together a Portfolio?

For the early years, your child's portfolio will contain samples of their best work from each subject and will include much Arts & Crafts, writing (prewriting/drawing) samples, photos of block or other structures they build, construction paper designs (apples from a paper apple tree of books read, for instance), pictures of field trips and anything else that will help you document their year. Even if you don't have the time to turn this into a professional-looking scrapbook, this documentation will reveal what your child learned over the year and will be filled with precious memories for your whole family.

From about Third Grade on, use plastic notebooks to keep track of their best work as much of the Arts & Crafts will be gone. Put in about five sheet protectors for each subject. Immediately after your child has produced superior work, place it in the child's portfolio. As better work is produced, just place it over the existing work (don't take the older work out). Keep a special cabinet in your home for the yearly portfolios as these will become more and more precious to you over time.

Make a portfolio for each grade that you school your child at home (whether by home schooling or by public school at home online such as through K12).

How Do I Assess My Student's Progress?

In order to truly assess your child's progress, you will need a professional assessment. If you're using an online curriculum provider such as K12, they will provide you with year-end testing.

There are online sites that offer free informal testing (www.freereading.net, math-and-reading-help-for-kids.org) but another home schooling alternative is to have Reading, Language Arts and Math testing done at your local for profit tutoring center. The testing will need to be done annually for your child beginning at the end of Third Grade (be sure to check your own state's regulations). These assessments will become part of your child's permanent home school records. Check your local regulations as to whether it is mandatory for you to submit a copy of the results to your local school district.

Even if it's not a mandatory requirement, it's still a good idea to know where your child is compared to others in his grade. What if you, unexpectedly, had to put him in school tomorrow? Would it be clear that he had been educated along your state's guidelines? There should be clear progress in his academics, even if he's running a couple of years behind due to a developmental delay.

What Do I Teach?

Go to your State's Department of Education web site and you should be able to locate the curriculum for your child's grade level. This only tells you what to teach; it doesn't tell you *how* to teach it. Also, the wording can make it difficult to guess exactly what the guideline specifies. Read the previous chapters in this book to gain valuable information that will guide in determining your child's needs.

If your child has never had a formal academic assessment, you will need to find out where they are in their development. Try out the activities for pre-Kindergarten (if appropriate). If they have difficulty, back up your attempts to the preschool level. If they have trouble with preschool, back them up to toddler. You get the idea.

Don't go by their age or grade level. Look for activities that are new and novel and that they are developmentally ready to learn. That makes learning fun and gives them confidence in themselves. You might want to keep notes for yourself that your child is doing Kindergarten math, but toddler language activities, for example.

Restrain yourself from (and don't let other people embarrass you into) pressuring your child needlessly by saying or thinking something along the lines of, "Oh, he should be doing this right now. Let's just hurry and catch him up fast or just jump to that level." My experience has been that your child needs each developmental step and, if he skipped one, you *will* be going back to fill in that blank at some point in time. As his skills (and possibly his language) improves, he will begin to learn faster and then, with fun multisensory games and activities (if you're willing to put in the time and effort), he will be able to catch up to his peers in many academic areas.

There are also many curriculum providers available and I would prefer that you use one if you can afford it. Creating a curriculum is a big job and having to make all of your own materials, buy workbooks, request books and videos from the library, etc., can turn it into an overwhelming job, not to mention you may miss important academic skills.

Another route is Study Island or the online testing practice system at your Board of Education web site. Study Island offers online lessons and practice questions that use games and scoring to motivate your child to learn and/or review. Please note that some children find Study Island very frustrating. Do not have your child retake a test he is repeatedly failing or it will be too difficult for him to ever bring up his score. Go over the lesson with him before he attempts to play the lesson games again.

> People have questioned me,
> **"Isn't that a lot of time and effort for just one child?"**
>
> (I can clearly see that this extra effort will make all the difference in the future for my child and our family.)
>
> **"Yes, it's worth it to *me* for just *my* child."**

What About My Special Needs Child?

If you have a special needs child, make friends with the Do2Learn web site, (do2learn.com,) which offers great special needs resources and songs.

Don't let a special needs diagnosis throw you. You'd be surprised how well things can turn out (even if they are not as you had originally envisioned).

Let me tell you a story about a mother and her two sons...

A mother's oldest son was diagnosed with autism when he was three and a half years old. She had another son too, 19 months younger, only the younger son was in a constant state of happy laughter and cheerfulness.

As the mother worried, fussed over, worked with, and cried over her autistic son, the happy little son watched his mother's work with his brother and began to learn quickly from the many activities (that his mother shared with him as well).

The happy little son was often neglected through lack of direct attention from his mother (who was focused on helping her son with difficulties).

Achieving Brilliance at Home

One night, when the happy son was still a baby, he became very ill and his mother agonized over trying to get him to take his bottle and she rocked him for hours. She cried and worried and loved her happy little baby more than she ever had before.

The first moral of this story is that a special needs child may very well bring out the best in you and cause you to love more deeply than you had realized was possible. The second moral is to watch out that you don't overlook a child who *is* capable, confident, and cheerful. The third moral is that, the more involved you are with a child, the more you develop a relationship with that child.

The Lord, in His boundless intelligence and love, knows what is best for you and your family. I can honestly tell you that a child with autism is equally as fascinating and loveable as a child that's gifted to their mother.

Do you *really* have a problem with your special needs child or do you feel like other people inflict shame and embarrassment upon you? Thank goodness, no one ever died from embarrassment, but they have died from their reaction to it. Just because some people in our society may give you and/or your child an assigned role, that doesn't mean you have to put it on like a raincoat.

On the other hand, show people compassion when they struggle to know how to act around you and your child. Imagine meeting someone from a completely different culture and who spoke a different language. It would take you a little while to adjust to your differences. It's that way with special needs kids.

Just give other people a little bit of time and you may be surprised to discover how wonderful most people really are at heart.

Jeanne Mifflin

About the Author

Jeanne Mifflin was a mother seeking ways to help her autistic son develop academic competence and reduce his learning frustration. This led her to home schooling where she soon realized that she'd captured the world for her son by using all of his senses during learning activities.

Researching all available information about how children learn and then creating and serving up multisensory games and activities for her son, Jeanne saw her autistic son (**and his gifted brother)** beginning to learn at an accelerated rate.

Fun and reinforcing activities (like a party after learning difficult skills) made sure that they were ready to try something new the next time.

Jeanne also grasped that many students struggle with math (as she had when she was growing up) and now realized how much easier it would have been for her to learn using a multisensory approach.

Based on years of personal experience, she utilizes two very basic principles: (1) If it's not fun, they're going to fight doing it; and (2) the more you know about something, the more interesting it becomes.

When Jeanne's autistic son was first diagnosed, he was placed in an autism preschool classroom through the public school system. She was able to observe a top-notch special education teacher work with her son and she immediately realized what an incredible difference a teacher could make in a student's capacity to learn and gain confidence in their own abilities.

She went on to research, study and utilize the best educational practices she could find as a home schooling parent (including the later use of the K12 curriculum). Whenever she tried to play "teacher," she noticed her sons would shut down. The auditory format that her gifted son thrived on seemed to leave her autistic son awash in an ocean of words. She then went on to discover that, given a choice, her gifted son rejoiced at being able to learn in a hands-on manner as well.

Jeanne discovered that, what worked well for her autistic son, worked well for all children.

Ability to Teach, 22

Acronyms, Educational, 45

Addition and Subtraction, 53

Addition, 119-120

Advantages, 15

Alien Astronaut Probe, 162

Alien Temperature Game, 155-157

Amazon Answer Guards, 173-174

Amazon Warrior Flash Cards, 170

Approach, 14

Area, 146, 149

Attendance Reporting, Home School, 214

Attitude, Home School, 209

Author, About the, 220

Averaging Numbers, 172

Bad Childhood Memories, 17

Bar Graphs and Pictographs, 54

Bedroom Cleaning, 33

Behavior, 19

Behavior Monitoring, 91

Block Spin, 169

Body, Using, 61

Celsius, 155

Chart, Pie, 176

Circle, 149

Cleaning, 33

College Degree, Lack of, 20

Colors Lesson, 80

Conflict Resolution, 56

Consequences, 97

Crawling, 66

Creating Your Own Materials, 103

Creative Development Goals, 57

Cross-Referencing Materials, 102

Cross-Subject Lesson Tree, 108

Curriculum, 44, 216

Danger, Greatest, 41

Decimals, 125

Decimals, Dividing, 135, 137

Decimals, Multiplying, 133, 136, 138

Decimals, Subtracting, 132

Directions, Giving, 32

Discouragement, 25

Division, 119

Do Say, 40

Don't Say, 40

Eating Problems, 74

Educational Acronyms, 45

Educational Jargon, 18

Educational Jargon, 44

Educational Vocabulary, 45

Emergency Preparedness, 86

Fahrenheit, 155

Family, 207

Fear, 16

Fear of Ridicule From Others, 17

Fear of Ridicule From Professional Teachers, 17

Fear We Will Teach Them the Wrong Way, 18

Field Trips, 203

Focus and Organization, 18

Fractions, 185

Fractions, Adding, 189-191

Fractions, Adding with Unlike Denominators, 192-194

Fractions, Converting Improper, 195-196

Fractions, Dividing, 197

Fractions, Equivalent, 187-188

Fractions, Multiplying, 196

Fruit Picked by Amazon Children, 172

Fun, Free, 199

Gallons, Quarts, Pints, 159

General Guidelines, 30

Geometry, 144

Geometry Curse Game, 147

Germs Rhyme, 78

Goal Setting, 29

Grams, 160

Graph, Bar, 179

Graph, Line, 180

Green Lesson Trees, 37

Hands, Using, 61, 69

Hercules Fraction Flip, 197

Holidays, 202

Home School, Reasons to, 207

Hygiene Skills, 86

Imitation, 70

Important, Emphasize the Most, 52

Independence, 21

Is It Worth It? 218

Judgment, Exercising Good, 51

Kitchen – Lesson 1, 38

Language, 65

Language, One and a Half, 70

Learning, 27

Learning Skills, 99

Learning Styles, 28

Least Common Denominator, 191

Legal Requirements, Home School 213

Legs, 65

Legs, Strengthen, 64

Lesson Creation, 35

Lesson Tree, 36

Lesson Tree, Inclusive, 110

Library, 200

Life Skills Goals (Adaptive), 57

Living Skills, 83, 86

Maps & Machines Goals, 56

Marital Problems, 20

Martian Bird's Eggs, 161

Martian Measurement, 158-159

Martian Stretch, 164

Math Ideas, Early, 77

Math Problem Solving, 112

Math, 62

Mean, Median & Mode, 171, 174

Measurement, 164

Measurement Goals, 54

Measurement, Martian, 158-159

Money, 19, 20

Money Goals, 54

Mother's Promise, Home School, 212

Multiplication, 119

My Bonnie Lies Over the Ocean, 79

Noun, Pronouns and Adjectives Song, 107

Nursery Rhymes Lesson, 82

One to Three Year Olds, 68

Party Ideas, 202

Perimeter, 146

Pharaoh's Tablet, 144

Physical Skills Goals, 57

Pi, 149

Place Value, 131

Play Skills, 86

Portfolio, 215

Potty Training, 74

Probability, 169

Probability & Statistics, 166, 182

Progress, 216

Progress, 24

Reading, 62, 108

Reading Ideas, Early, 75

Relation Words, 53

Resources, 89

Reward Ideas, 95

Roll Backward, 65

Roll Forward, 65

Routine, 94

Salt Dough Recipe, 162

Sample Lesson, 79

Schedule Example, Summer, 101

Schedule, 58

Schedule, Young Child, 98

Science, 62, 78, 109

Science Goals, 57

Seven Continents Song, 78

Shapes & Sizes Goals, 55

Shapes Lesson, 81

Shapes Review, 145

Sitting, 63

Sitting at the Table, 84

Six Months to a Year, 63

Sleeping Through the Night, 67

Social Skills, 78

Social Studies, 62, 108

Social Studies Ideas, 79

Social Studies – People, 56

Social Studies – Personal Responsibility, 55

Societal Pressure, 19

Solid Food, 67

Songs and Poems, 72

Speaking, 61

Special Needs, 218

Standing, Pull Up to, 64

Stores, 201

Strange Coincidences Game, 182

Structure, 94

Subtraction, 119

Swing, 1950's, 164

Teach, What to, 95

Teaching Materials, 41

Theme Parks, 204

Things to Come, 61

Three to Seven Year Olds, 75

Time Management, 83

Time Management, Games for, 34

Time Zone Take-Off, 162

Tree Diagram, 175

Twinkle, Twinkle, Little Star, 71

Viewing Reels, 108

Walking, 69

Word Problems, 121

Writing, 104

Writing, 108

Yes/No, 65

Made in the USA
Charleston, SC
09 March 2015